It's Not My Fault!

-or-

Can a Rabbi's Son Find Happiness
as a Tennis Pro?

It's Not My Fault!

-or-
Can a Rabbi's Son Find Happiness as a Tennis Pro?

Daniel I. Waintrup, MBA

www.AcanthusPublishing.com

Acanthus Publishing
a division of The Ictus Group LLC

Publisher's Cataloging-In-Publication Data
(Prepared by The Donohue Group, Inc.)

Waintrup, Daniel I.
It's not my fault, or, Can a rabbi's son find happiness as a tennis pro? / by
Daniel I. Waintrup.

p. : ill. ; cm.
ISBN-13: 978-0-9754810-7-3
ISBN-10: 0-9754810-7-X

1. Waintrup, Daniel I. 2. Tennis players--United States--Biography. 3. Tennis
coaches--United States--Biography. 4. Jewish men--United States--Biography.
5. Jewish wit and humor. I. Title. II. Title: Can a rabbi's son find happiness as
a tennis pro?

GV994.W35 W35 2005
796.342/092

Printed in the United States of America
10 9 8 7 6 5 4 3 2 1

Designed by Charisse L. Brookman
Cover Photos by Jay O'Brien
Illustrations by Dan Rosandich

Dedication

To my wife Linda, to Talor, Rebecca, Kimberly and Samantha, to Debby and Miriam, to my parents, my in-laws, and my entire family, and to everyone who has helped me achieve this important goal.

Contents

Acknowledgements

This book is the culmination of a dream. I have actually been writing it off and on for over twenty years. It was the convergence of several events that caused me to finally bring this baby to life. The most important of these are things that have happened to me below the surface – subtle changes that have caused me to think differently about purpose, accomplishment, and fulfillment. I can honestly say, as I put the final touches on this manuscript, that it's been a helluva ride so far, but the best is yet to come.

I want to thank the thousands of unique, often crazy, always interesting adult and junior students I've had the privilege to teach over the years, who have provided me with the inspiration for much of the material in this book.

I'd like to acknowledge the contribution of my editor, Paige Stover Hague, for giving me the motivation to finally complete this project and for being instrumental in its organization and development.

I would like to thank the CEO of the investment company for whom I work, for creating a job that has allowed me the freedom to write this book, despite telling me recently, "I'd really prefer it if people didn't know that you work for the company. We'll just keep it our little secret – but I do love you, big guy…"

I want to acknowledge my (real) shrink, for all the support and guidance he's given me over the years, although he told me recently, after I invited him to the book signing party, that for "professional reasons" he'd prefer it if people didn't know that we'd been working together for the past ten years.

I want to thank all of my friends for their unyielding encouragement during the entire project, especially my good friend Bill, who, in a characteristic show of confidence in my abilities and this book, told me, "The only way you'll ever sell that thing is door to door, buddy!"

And last, but not least, I wish to acknowledge my wife, Linda, for her patience and compassion during this entire project, despite telling me on more than one occasion that she had her divorce attorney on speed dial if she didn't like how she was portrayed.

X

Daniel Waintrup
Brookline, MA
July 2005

1. The Great Catch

I am eight years old. It's near dusk in late July. I'm the
youngest member of my summer camp's junior varsity
softball team. The coach has me playing right field and
is secretly hoping and praying that I won't see a lot of
action. I'm known as the funny kid here at camp, not
the superstar right fielder. It's the bottom of the ninth;
the biggest game of the summer, the annual intra-camp
competition, and it feels like the whole world is watching. My team is leading, one to nothing, and there are
two outs. The bases are loaded and our hated opponents
have their cleanup hitter at the plate.

My mind starts to wander. "God, it's hot out here... I
want a drink of water. Is that my entire bunk watching?
Wow... I can't wait to jump into the pool when this
game is over..."

Suddenly, I hear the crack of the bat. The hitter has smacked a line drive into the right-centerfield gap. I take off like a shot and run for what seems like an eternity, sprinting as hard as I can. I dive for the ball. I am rolling, sliding, tumbling, grabbing. I have it! I don't! I have it – maybe. I am flat on the ground grasping with the glove. Is it in the glove or on the ground? Can't see – dirt and sweat and hair are in my eyes. Without a rational thought, I grab the ball and thrust it high in the air.

"I got it! I got it!" I scream.

Running out onto the field to make the call, the umpire agrees. "Yer out! That's the ball game! Helluva catch, kid. Helluva catch!"

2

But had I really caught the ball?

Before I can grapple with this complex question, my fellow campmates swarm the field and carry me off, ecstatic that we've defeated our bitter rivals.

"Great catch, Danny, baby – unbelievable! You won the game for us, baby; you won the game!" my coach, who is also my favorite camp counselor, cries promising me free canteen for the rest of the summer.

"Hey, Danny, you were great out there. I'll see you tonight at the big dance," echoes Molly Goldman, the cute little blonde who I'd had a crush on all summer.

"This hero stuff ain't bad," I think to myself.

But that one nagging question still persists. Had I really caught the ball? The reality of the matter was that I just wasn't sure. One thing that I *was* certain of, however, was that it was too late to change anyone's mind. I was the camp hero, the toast of the town, and I was loving my newfound notoriety! There wasn't a replay tape to review in 1964.

As I look back on this episode now, after years of intense work with my favorite therapist (some of you may be familiar with him; his name – Jack Daniel's), I find it amazing how I reacted on that fateful afternoon. Would a more honest individual have admitted that he actually dropped the ball? I was a rabbi's son for christsakes; would I rot in hell for this transgression?

However, I did learn one crucial lesson from this impor-tant event: If indeed I hadn't caught the ball, I was certainly one of the most natural, instinctive liars that ever lived. And if this was true, how could I best apply this ability to "stretch the truth" later in life? Companies like Enron and WorldCom didn't exist back in the '60s and the '70s when I was growing up. I couldn't aspire to work for a business like that. Become a CPA? I just didn't see myself fabricating revenue numbers for some Fortune 500 company or developing complex fraudulent accounting schemes.

3

Used car salesman? My mother would never allow it, and besides, being Jewish, I barely knew how to turn the goddamn things on!

And, please, law school was out of the question. So, the issue remained: How was I going to use this God-given ability? For a long time I couldn't sort this out. Then one day I picked up a tennis racquet and beat my best friend, who had been playing for five years. I had found my calling.

And of course, the rest is history…

"Yes, Mrs. Lebowitz, I know that's the twentieth forehand in a row that you've hit over the back fence, but the last two only cleared the top by ten feet. I think you're really improving, bubby!"

Years later, during my country club teaching career, my son raised a most interesting question as he watched me "instruct" another satisfied client.

4

"Hey, Dad, what if what happened to Jim Carrey in *Liar Liar* happened to you sometime?" he postulated. "Wouldn't that be hysterical?"

"A most interesting question," I thought to myself. What if, as with Jim Carrey in the movie, a spell was cast on me that made me unable to tell a lie for an entire day? Would my students be able to handle "the truth," or would it be our collective worst nightmare? That night, as I lay tossing and turning in bed, unable to sleep, grappling with this troubling question, I imagined what it might be like.

My normal Mrs. Lebowitz instruction: "Honey, you're playing so well today! You're playing spectacularly! I don't think I've ever seen you move better or hit the ball so solidly!"

Teaching the same student without the normal "positive reinforcement":

"Sweetheart, let's face it, YOU'RE AWFUL! You know it, I know it, the club knows it, and the world knows it! Why waste each other's time? I know the perfect sport for you: BASKET WEAVING!"

Of course, I could only imagine what it might be like to teach my oldest student, ninety-year-old Mo Weinberg.

My usual instruction: "Mo, you're doing unbelievably well today. We just hit three forehands in a row before you had to stop and use the respirator! I see real progress here, young man!"

And the slight differences when being instructed by the "truthful" tennis pro:

"Mo, Mo, Mo… We both know that unless I hit the ball right at you, you're not going to get it. YOU'RE NINETY YEARS OLD, BUBBY! Do me a favor – the gin game's upstairs!"

As others have pointed out over the years, much of my country club teaching involved lessons with extremely wealthy and powerful CEOs of Fortune 500 companies. I was almost afraid to imagine the possibilities.

The normal me: "Wow! You're hammering the ball today, Mr. Levine! Are you going to pass me every time I come to net? I may have to start paying you for these lessons!"

But without my usual positive attitude, I don't think Mr. CEO would be offering me a position in his company anytime soon.

"Another forehand error – what a surprise. That makes ten in the first set alone! You may drive a Bentley, big guy, but that don't make a difference out here, does it? By the way, how's that SEC investigation going?"

I spent fifteen years – some of the best in my life – as a teaching pro at one of the most prestigious country clubs in New England. Following a fairly impressive college career, I was a ranked player in the '80s and '90s, and in 2005 (as I am about to turn fifty) I won the men's singles championships at the Palm Beach Country Club on a blistering day – but you'll hear more about that later.

I grew up in Abington, Pennsylvania, the son of a highly respected rabbi and rebbitzen – both of whom held influential positions in our community. I have two older sisters who alternately tortured and ignored me, which contributed significantly to the building of my character and the development of my ability to charm and/or amuse just about anyone I wanted to. I had a fairly conventional upbringing, for a rabbi's son, which has resulted in my being no more screwed up than your average child of the '70s – it was not a pretty era (Inagodadavita, honey…).

6

I learned that I was an exceptional tennis player almost by accident. I was fast, I was great defensively, and I learned that I could go very far just holding my own and waiting for my opponent to blink. Wasn't that a life lesson! Oh, if I only knew now what I didn't know then.

My story unfolds in the pages that follow, told from several perspectives. I beg the reader's indulgence in telling what some might label a "vanity" expression, but I offer no apology, because I think you will see I'm more than willing to be the object of the joke when it's deserved. Interspersed throughout these chapters I have included some instructional tennis tips, which are intended to assist you in developing skill and style on the court. Most importantly, however, they are intended to help you acquire the attitude of winning, because as you will discover in the pages that follow, I have learned a few things about playing to win. I haven't always done it the conventional way, but I generally end the match in the winner's box. As such, I invite you to join me for a brief telling of the story of my life, so far…

Letters to the Country Club Tennis Pro

As one of the best (in my mind), the baldest (in everybody's mind), and the busiest (in my dreams) country club tennis teaching professionals in the country, I've found it next to impossible to answer the multitude of questions my students might have before, during, or after an hour of instruction. So, at my club I created "Dear Mr. Country Club Tennis Pro," a system where individual students, regular club members, or anyone else could jot down their questions about any aspect of tennis or the pro, submit them, and have them answered by me personally. I have sprinkled a selection of these throughout the book. Enjoy.

8

Dear Mr. Country Club Tennis Pro,

I was watching you play yesterday, and you remind me a lot of the great John McEnroe when he was on tour. I bet you could give him a hell of a match if you really wanted to!

Signed,
Harry

Dear Harry,

Whatever medication you're on, I strongly suggest you
double the dosage! I wouldn't have a chance in a match
against Johnny Mac! In general, the differences between a
teaching pro and touring pro competitively, economically,
mentally, etc., are far too numerous to mention. But before
they put you away, I've listed some of the major differences
between us, so you can get a better grip on reality.

	John Patrick McEnroe	Daniel (country club pro) Waintrup
Annual income:	$5 million	$50,000
Career:	4 US Open titles 3 Wimbledon titles	Semi-finals Newark Invitational
Cars:	2 Porsches 3 Mercedes	'83 Datsun (passenger door does not open)
Houses:	Manhattan French Riviera Aspen, Malibu	Ray and Gloria's Trailer Park
Last Tourney:	ATP Stuttgart (world champs)	Rogaine Invitational
Last Book Read:	*Investing Your Millions*	*Shooting Craps Vegas Style*

9

Dear Mr. Country Club Tennis Pro,

My wife and I really enjoy playing
in the club championships every
year. What do you feel is the most
important factor that contributes
to the successful organization and
completion of this event?

Signed,
Robert Hertzberg

Dear Robert,

In my opinion, the most important factor in running a successful country club tennis tournament is the establishment of playing categories that your country club clientele can relate to. I've listed below the sign-up sheets from my last event.

Men making over
$250,000/yr

1. _____
2. _____

Men making over
$1,000,000/yr

1. _____
2. _____

Men making over
$500,000/yr

1. _____
2. _____

Men recently filing
Chapter 11

1. _____
2. _____

Women unwilling to
run more than one step

1. _____
2. _____

Women unwilling to
run more than two
steps

1. _____
2. _____

Women unwilling to
run more than three
steps

1. _____
2. _____

Women who'd
prefer to have their au
pair run for them

1. _____
2. _____

Dear Mr. Country Club Tennis Pro,

I watched you give a lesson to Mrs. Abramawitz the other day, and I couldn't believe how she didn't stop talking and how many questions she asked you. I mean, I don't think you hit ten balls with her the entire hour! Does this happen often here at the club?

Signed,
Roger

Dear Roger,

Many of the students I work with at the country club are talkative and extremely inquisitive. It's interesting to note, now that you mention it, of all the millions of questions that I've been asked in my country club teaching career, how certain ones keep popping up:

1) "Who's your therapist?"
2) "What are you really going to do with the rest of your life?"
3) "Would you like to borrow some of my Propecia?"
4) "When are you going to get a real job?"
5) "Does it bother you much that your parents decided to change their last name after you became a tennis pro?"

Dear Mr. Country Club Tennis Pro,

I saw your son playing here at the country club today and he looks just like you! Does he have a similar tennis game also?

Signed,
Michelle Guttman

Dear Michelle,

Actually, it's pretty amazing. My son does look like his old man a little bit, doesn't he? He even has that nice, steady, consistent tennis game like his dear old dad. But, Michelle, I have to admit – and this is a little depressing – he doesn't drink, doesn't smoke, doesn't chase women – WHERE DID I GO WRONG?!

Dear Mr. Country Club Tennis Pro,

I was shocked and outraged the other day after watching the parents of one of your top students screaming at their child for not playing well and losing his match. I mean, what kind of idiots are these people? The kid was sobbing his eyes out! Isn't it wrong to put so much pressure on any child when he or she competes? I'm sure you'll be a lot more compassionate with your kids!

Signed,
Concerned Charlie

Dear Charlie,

It's extremely important for parents not to put an excessive amount of pressure on their children when they compete. Unfortunately, as you observed, there are many adults who place too much of an emphasis on winning and losing, and not enough importance on having their kids just go out, do the best they can, play hard, and have a good time.

In terms of my own children, I don't care whether they win or lose when they come off a tennis court as long as they give 100 percent and enjoy themselves. I don't even care what sport they play! They could end up playing football or basketball or hockey – it doesn't matter to me. I mean, my kids know they don't have to end up playing tennis just because their father is a tennis pro. Just last week, my son told me he wanted to join the lacrosse team, and I told him that he can play any sport he wants, whether it's singles, doubles, mixed doubles, or Canadian doubles – whatever he wants. I'm totally open-minded!

The Son Interjects

Unlike my dad, I don't lie. I am a first-degree black belt in Kenpo karate and an instructor at the school as well. Ethical behavior is the foundation of my personality. The underlying values of karate are modesty, courtesy, integrity, self-control, perseverance, and a certain spirit that distinguishes character. Karate students hold their heads high, above all else.

"Wow!" was my reaction to "The Great Catch." The story pretty much sums up the difference between Dad and me. To this day, he doesn't know if he caught the ball or not, but that didn't matter to him. He was a hero after that game, and I think the juices in his brain kind of took off, telling him that he was good at this thing called "stretching the truth." And if you got a talent, you should use it, right?

All I'm saying is if I were in the same situation, I probably would have confessed to missing the ball, because of my karate background. I have to admit, and my dad might be just a bit too excited over this, that if I weren't schooled in karate, I probably would have done the same thing and screamed, "I got it! I got it!"

My dad and I joke about everything. It's the essence of our relationship. After twenty years with Daniel Isaac Waintrup, I've learned he loves to lie. But there are those rare times when he tells it like it is. My dad likes to liven up a situation up with humor. A lot of that comes from his childhood, because he was always a funny guy growing up. People were and still are drawn to him because of his comedic nature. There's no getting around it. My grandfather was the rabbi in the town, who everyone knew and loved. Humor comes naturally to my father because his father, the rabbi, is also a very funny person. They both like to have fun.

Dad has done a lot of crazy things that we won't discuss in print. After all, he is the hero of this little story. And sometimes he crosses the line and beats a joke to death. But I'll forgive him for that. He means well… I think.

I will, however, suggest that he is a little too eager to disclose his amorous exploits. Why does he need to share? I prefer to be a little more discreet in this department. He wonders where he went wrong because I don't smoke, I don't drink, and I don't chase women. Well he's absolutely right on the first two counts. As to the third, I've found that allowing oneself to be chased, rather than chasing, can sometimes lead to more meaningful results. All I can say is that college life is *great!* I've told you that before, Daddy-o.

15

Dad, I can confidently say, you're one in a million. Ha!

Waintrup's Rules for Winning
Learn to Play Better Tennis "NOW!"

Tennis is, and always will be, a game of reaction. If you want to play the game at its highest level and to your fullest potential as a player, you have to be consciously and consistently aware of when to start moving for your opponent's shot during a rally. I always try to explain to my students the importance of movement on a tennis court, that if you want to be a really good player, you have to be ready to start moving for your opponent's shot the second it comes off his or her racquet.

Over the years, I've found one of the most effective ways to demonstrate this reaction process is visually. I have my students watch one of my assistant pros play a point with me. I have them notice how we are on the balls of our feet during the rally and how our eyes are fixed on the area of each other's "hitting zone," which allows us to quickly react to shots the instant they come off the racquet.

Being "on your toes" during a point gives you the greatest possible chance to react quickly in any direction; it gives you the greatest possible chance to start moving and start reacting to the speed, spin (or lack thereof), and direction of the shot, so you can get in position to return it. Of course, getting some of my country club students to bounce on their toes is not always the easiest of tasks. Sometimes, I have to compromise a little bit:

"Okay, okay. I know you just had the pedicure, so bounce lightly. Bounce lightly on your toes. Work with me here, bubby! Work with me!"

For those students who can't quite grasp this concept of reaction from a visual demonstration, I find that some of them will respond to this idea "verbally."

I rally with them and yell "NOW!" when this important reaction process is ideally supposed to begin. For many people, the sound of my voice is a better trigger to get them to recognize when their eyes and their brains are supposed to start tracking their opponents' shots so they can get in position to make a return. Over time, I have these students internalize this process by saying "Now!" or "React!" or "Move your lazy butt, you idiot!" to themselves during a rally with friends or during a match - whatever gets them to move and understand that if they want to have any chance of being a consistent tennis player, they have

17

to be consciously aware of when to start moving for the ball.

Learning to play better tennis "NOW!" has been an effective instructional tool for this country club teaching professional over the years. Giving students a visual or auditory signal of when to react on a tennis court is also a great way to get the point across that if they want to play to their fullest potential, they have to know when to start moving for their opponent's shot. For those students who don't see the necessity or relevance of moving or reacting on a tennis court, I have this advice for them:

"Hey, bubby, the first tee's across the street. Have a good round!"

Truthfully, I've always felt a little empathy for my fellow golf teaching professionals. I could never imagine a more difficult, more complex, more unforgiving sport to try to teach, especially to a student with limited coordination. The stark, cold reality of the sport is that a golf pro can talk until he or she is blue in the face, can try to get the point across with humor or analogies or anecdotes or videotapes or with every conceivable teaching technique in the book – but at the end of the day, the students have little chance to succeed if they don't possess the ability to swing that long, narrow club with the little, tiny face and the little, tiny hitting area and make contact with that little, tiny ball.

My own frustration with the game of golf is blatantly obvious when I watch the big boys playing some major event on TV, and I hear the announcer say, "Tiger's about 290 yards away, downwind, behind a tree, in a creek, next to a rock. Easy nine iron!"

Gimme a break!

The golf pro will never have the advantage of the tennis pro, who can give his or her student a really big racquet with a really big hitting area and feed or hit a perfectly-placed, really big ball about waist high, with little speed and no spin, to an area where the student is bound to make contact and have a positive learning experience.

I've spent the majority of my country club teaching career trying to convince golfers to play tennis. Over the years, it's gotten easier and easier.

19

I used to stand in the golf pro shop and wait for the frequently depressed, usually frustrated, and often overweight golfers to come off the eighteenth green.

"Hey, Fred, how'd you play today?"

"Terrible. Just terrible. I don't know why I bother. I take lessons, I practice — one minute I'm a star, the next minute I can't hit the ball. It's driving me crazy!"

"Yeah, I know, I know, tough game. Hey, Fred, I know a great sport you can play. It's exponentially easier, unbelievably more forgiving, doesn't take five hours to play – you can play it in an hour for godsakes – and to top it off, you can get a great aerobic workout, maybe lose a few of those extra pounds."

"You're right. I've been meaning to call you! Hey, what are you doing tomorrow morning?"

"Playing tennis with you, bubby. Playing tennis with you. See you at eight!"

Like taking candy from a baby.

Dear Mr. Country Club Tennis Pro,

If you had to name the single most important thing you need in order to be a better tennis player, what would it be?

Signed,
Harry Gold

Dear Harry,

As we say in the business, if you have money, you can improve! And if you don't, well, bubby, it's not my fault!

Even at a young age, little Danny
Waintrup loved his foie gras.

#2.

Moments after this picture was
taken, Danny ran away from home
and had a religious experience.

"Like most people from Philadelphia, I've been addicted to Tastykakes since I was a young boy."

"Maybe I could have been a better football player if someone would have taught me how to zip up my fly."

2. Growing Up in the Rabbi's House

Dear Mr. Country Club Tennis Pro,

Did your parents really get upset when
you told them you wanted to become a
tennis pro and play the world professional
tour, or is that just an exaggeration?

Signed,
Curious Carol

Dear Carol,

Not only did my parents not support my decision to
become a teaching pro and attempt to play the world
tour, my father tried to strangle me with his talles eight
or nine times. My parents' idea of a successful career
for me was not playing some Swede in LA one week and
then some big Czech in Monte Carlo the next. It was
working in my Uncle Perry's law firm in Chicago and
collecting a big check! (See photograph #8, pg. 50.)

Dear Mr. Country Club Tennis Pro,

I just got through playing a match with you, and let me tell you, buddy, you may have won, but every legitimate tennis player in the world knows that a guy like you who just pushes and dinks and slices every single ball will never, ever get past a certain level competitively! All you do is slice, slice, slice! What's the matter? Don't you know how to hit a topspin drive? Are you afraid to hit the ball like a man? Aren't big-time tennis pros like yourself supposed to be able to drive the ball offensively?

Signed,
Frustrated Freddy

Dear Frustrated Freddy,

I'd really like to hit up on the ball and put some topspin into my game, but I really can't help myself. The slicing, chopping, high to low motion just seems so natural to me. Maybe it's hereditary. You know, my father's not just a rabbi; he's also a *Mohel!*

Lessons the Rabbi Taught Me

There were a lot of good times and a lot of laughs growing up as the son of Rabbi Harold Bernard Waintrup. I mean, let's face facts, my father is not what you would call your "typical" rabbi. By typical, I mean the traditional, centuries-old image of the somber, serious-minded, conservative-thinking, Torah-studying leader of the Jewish community. Believe me, my father is anything but that guy! Truthfully, there were probably more than a few people in his congregation who felt Rabbi Waintrup had maybe studied "a little too much Talmud," if you know what I mean. I have always wondered, "Did I really even have any chance of growing up normal?"

Until I was sixteen years old, my friends would call the house looking for me, only to have my father pick up the phone and, in his best British accent, inform them, "Daniel isn't available to speak right now because he's taking his milk bath, but I'm certain after his massage he could give you a call back."

27

The next day my friends would ask, "Who was that guy who answered the phone last night at your house?"

And I'd answer, "Oh, that's my old man. He thinks he's Henny Youngman. Now do you understand me a little better?!"

You see, my father always dreamed of being an actor and believed that going to New York or Hollywood to pursue work on the stage or in film was his ultimate calling. He fantasized about being a stand-up comic, the next Henny

Youngman. This was, however, just the tip of the iceberg as to what it was like growing up with my father.

Another joke my father loved to play on me occurred many mornings before school. Often the first thing I would hear at 6 a.m. would be the Rabbi serenading me with some old, obscure Jewish melody. I can only hope and pray that most people in their lives never have to experience the shock of waking up to their father singing "Come Light the Menorah Candle." I truly believe that many of the nervous twitches and psychotic tendencies I have to this day can be traced back to these moments. Of course, the best was yet to come.

On those mornings, I'd wearily drag myself down to the kitchen for the breakfast he had prepared for me. After a few moments of trying to eat my Cheerios and milk, I'd notice something strange; I wasn't getting any milk with my cereal. As confusion crossed my face, I would look across the table to see my father, a grown man, a noted Talmudic scholar, and respected leader of Old York Road Temple Beth Am, laughing hysterically, tears rolling down his face, pounding his fist on the table in sheer delight. The Rabbi had once again gotten me with his famous "holy spoon" routine.

Every once in a while, I have been able to give back to the Rabbi as good as I got it. One of my greatest comebacks followed a little incident, which is now legendary in my family:

They say I was extremely hyper as a child. In my mind, I just wanted a little attention. Problem was, I wasn't

28

getting much on a very hot Mother's Day in 1959. Little three-year-old Danny Waintrup wanted to play with someone; he wanted some action, but there was nobody around. My father was writing a sermon and my mother was cooking dinner. I have no idea where my sisters were. The only thing I knew was that I was hungry for some candy and wanted some entertainment.

"I know where to go," I remember thinking to myself. "I'll go down to the Abington Pharmacy. I really like it there!"

And so I did.

Now, it should be pointed out that my destination was almost a half-mile away and would necessitate crossing an extremely busy street. Of course, when you're three years old, these don't appear to be major obstacles.

It was time for dinner and my parents soon noticed that I wasn't in my room. They frantically searched the house and the backyard. They couldn't find me and asked some of the neighbors for help. My sisters and friends joined the search, but I was nowhere to be found. Soon the police were called – and the fire department and National Guard. The Rabbi and his wife were really freaking out. Had I been abducted? Had I run away? Had I gone for a walk in the woods and gotten lost?

One person was completely unaware of all the commotion surrounding my disappearance, and that was little Danny Waintrup. He was extremely happy, sitting on the floor of the Abington Pharmacy, hungrily munching on some Hershey's Kisses from a bag he had broken open, and reading his favorite Archie comic books. Fortunately, the pharmacist noticed this young boy sitting all alone and recognized the nametag on the back of his shirt. He called my house and the search was called off.

To say that my family was relieved is a slight understatement.

"I'll never understand how you were able to cross that busy street on your own," I can still hear my father saying to me at the time.

In later years, I seized this opportunity to pay him back for all the laughs and practical jokes he had had at my expense.

"Jesus helped me cross that road, Rabbi."

"What?"

"It was Jesus! Praised be the Lord!"

"Please don't…"

"He took me by the hand; He reached out to me; He helped me across that busy street."

"I think you're a little confused, son. We don't believe…"

"He reached out to me, Rabbi. I'd been forsaken by you – cast aside, ignored. I was all alone, standing on the edge, and then Christ reached out to me and brought me across that difficult divide."

"I think I'm going to be sick."

"Praised be His name! The Son of God saved my life! You should be eternally grateful, Rabbi."

"I think I'm going to be eternally nauseous. Please don't repeat this to anyone in the congregation. Think of my reputation, son."

"Of course, my father. But you know, everything in life has a price."

"How much is it going to cost me?"

31

"Just a $35 raise in my weekly allowance."

"Jesus Christ!"

"Yes, Rabbi, yes! Praised be His name." (See photograph #2, pg. 22.)

I think the most important gift my father has given me is the ability to laugh and to make other people laugh. I've always wondered, could there ever be a more valuable character trait than having the ability to make other people happy? Could there ever be anything as important as being able to loosen up a potential new client with a little humor; or being able to "break the ice" with a joke in a tense, uncomfortable social situation; or simply having the ability to get your son or daughter to see the lighter side of a situation when they're feeling a little down or depressed? In my mind, I truly think there isn't. My father not only gave me this innate ability, this natural sense of irreverence, but he also taught me how to laugh at myself, to not take myself too seriously. In essence, he showed me how to stay positive and maintain a sense of humor when times were difficult. For this, I will always be grateful.

What was it like growing up as the son of a rabbi in Abington, Pennsylvania in the '60s and '70s? Well, I certainly realized early on that I was a little different from the rest of the "guys" in the neighborhood. I realized this most painfully on the very first Christmas I can remember. I was probably eight or nine years old and my father, through some quirk of fate – or as I like to think, some latent, sadistic, rabbinical need to punish me in some way – decided to buy a home in an almost completely non-Jewish neighborhood, on a street corner surrounded by a number of large Catholic and Protestant families. Indeed, many of the kids I grew up playing sports and games with were from these families, and I certainly have my share of fond memories of them.

But not on this day. It was Christmas morning and I can still remember little Danny Waintrup wandering over to his living room window, clutching his pair of black socks and the small, plastic dreidel his parents had so generously given him for Chanukah a few weeks before, tearfully watching twenty or thirty of his closest friends running and jumping and laughing with delight. Christmas had come and they had hit the motherload! It was Mardi Gras in Abington and this rabbi's son was definitely not going to be part of the celebration.

As I watched my "friends" playing outside with their planes, trains, baseball gloves, and Erector Sets, I was jealous of all the new things they had. I was depressed about all the things I didn't get on my holiday. Tears rolling down my face, hands clutching my little dreidel, I knew my father would help me in my time of need.

"Have your mother make you some potato latkes with applesauce. That will make you feel better, son!"

I think times like these contributed to the rebellious streak in me. In my opinion, you can't get more rebellious than a young boy leaving his Hebrew school class during Passover, crossing the street from the synagogue where his father is the rabbi, and eating a cheeseburger at McDonald's. (I always seemed to have a little trouble with that *matzah* thing.)

33

Of course, this act of rebellion seems tame when compared to a rabbi's daughter I knew who vehemently resented the conservative-thinking, highly-religious, Israel-supporting nature of her father and the "Jewish" life he wanted her to live. She made it a point not only to date Arabs, but to let him know about it whenever she could! ("Muhammed and I had a great time at the dance, Daddy!")

Like a lot of R.K.s (Rabbis' kids) that I knew in my life, I really wanted to push the envelope as far as I could. My main goal in life during my teenage years was to see if I could date every great-looking *shiksah* in town. And you know what, I think I came pretty close.

When my father would ask me who I was going out with on Saturday night, I never quite had the heart to tell him.

"What are you doing tonight, son?"

"I got a hot date, Dad."

"With whom?"

"You don't know her – great girl, Stacey Smith…berg – you know, great family."

"Smithberg… Unusual name. They belong to Temple Shalom?"

"Oh, Dad, I'm not sure. But don't worry, I'll be sure to ask her."

However, as much as I often rebelled against the idea of being a rabbi's son, I certainly didn't mind some of the benefits that often came with the title – like being able to date any girl in my father's congregation if the "*shiksah* well" was running a little dry.

"Mr. Goldberg, how are you? Is Jennifer ready?"

"Daniel, my boy, come in! How are you? Have something to eat. Stay for awhile."

"No, I'd love to, but we're late for the movie and…"

"How's the Rabbi? Everything okay?"

"Sure, great, never better."

"Loved the sermon Friday night. I didn't see you at Temple."

"No, I couldn't make it. Did you say Jennifer was almost ready to…"

"Sure, sure. Hey, what kind of car are you driving?"

"Well, it's just a secondhand Buick that I…"

"Take my car! Just bought it; drives like a charm."

"No, I couldn't. I wouldn't feel right."

"Please, such a nice boy, the Rabbi's son. It's a *mitzvah;* take it – take my daughter for as long as you want. Have some fun!"

Like I said, growing up as a rabbi's son definitely had its perks!

Growing up as a Jew in suburban Philadelphia during this time period was certainly not all fun and games. I felt once again that my father chose to punish me – or maybe he was just trying to make me "mentally tougher," you know, like in that Johnny Cash song, "A Boy Named Sue" – by choosing to become a Rabbi in the town next to the town with all the Jews! When my high school played the next town over in football, the chant at the pep rally was how we were really going to "Beat those Jews!"

Just as important as learning to laugh and make other people laugh was inheriting the Rabbi's great athletic ability and hand-eye coordination. My father showed enough athletic promise in his early years to be invited to the Cleveland Indians training camp. (See photograph #6, pg. 49.) But, as he's often said, he chose the rabbinate over professional baseball, preferring to make "his hit from the pulpit."

I was somewhat shy and introverted at an early age, but being good at almost any sport was my ticket to social involvement in the real world, the world beyond my father's congregation. I don't think it's possible to overestimate the importance, especially as one of the youngest kids in the neighborhood (and as one of its only Jews), of always being included in the neighborhood's baseball, basketball, and football games.

To this day, I believe that I chose to play tennis over the other major sports because all my Jewish friends were playing tennis. On the tennis court, I knew that I wouldn't have to deal with the anti-Semitic comments I encountered trying out for the baseball, basketball, and football teams. The prevalence of these subtle and not-so-subtle attitudes caused some of my friends and me to form our own sports team – the Jewish All-Stars. We played football and softball against other groups in the area, and after a few wins we were feeling pretty good about ourselves. Then we accepted a challenge from a team on the other side of town to a game of tackle football. Unfortunately, we found out on the day of the game that the majority of the "guys" we were up against happened to be starters on their high school team. After the game, during which most of my brethren sustained cracked ribs, severe ankle sprains, and painful groin pulls, I made certain to point this out to my fellow All-Stars: "Boys, look on the bright side. We learned an important lesson today: Jews don't play in football games, we own the teams!"

Yeah, I owe my old man a lot. I think one of the things that I'm most thankful for is that he never forced me to do anything that I didn't want to do. (Well, with the exception of threatening my life if I didn't marry a Jewish girl!) Although he would always joke about how "there's still time to get into the rabbinic seminary," he never made any judgments on the career paths I chose, never made any demands on me as to what he thought I should do with my life.

37

The only thing he ever asked of me is that no matter what I chose to do with my life, I work hard at it and give it 100 percent, always keep a positive attitude, and respect others as I would want others to respect me.

The last thing my father gave me is something that I'll always, always, always be grateful for: low cholesterol! On those evenings when my friends are forced to eat halibut or chicken or sushi, I'm savoring sautéed foie gras, California Cabernet, filet mignon smothered with béarnaise sauce, a large portion of mushroom risotto, and white truffles. On these evenings, people sometimes hear me whisper, "Thank you, Rabbi Waintrup. Thank you so much!"

Yeah, I owe my old man a lot. But the eternal joke between us is that he owes me something, too. Specifically, my Bar Mitzvah money! May 14, 1969. I remember the date of my Bar Mitzvah like it was yesterday. My father gave me the most lines to chant from the Torah in the history of Old York Road Beth Am, and I didn't make one mistake. I also remember counting up all the money after the party. It must have been at least $2,000. So, Rabbi, where is the Bar Mitzvah money?

"Don't worry, my son, it's in a safe place."

"But, Rabbi, where's the Bar Mitzvah money?"

"The Lord moves in mysterious ways, my son."

"I'll tell you one thing, big guy. You'll be moving in mysterious ways – in prison."

"Who would've ever thought you could have it in your heart to make such a wonderful gift?"

"Please, don't tell me – you didn't…"

"You did, my son."

"My two-grand!"

"The land of Abraham, Isaac, and Jacob will always be grateful."

"I could've bought a car with that dough!"

"I can't tell you how proud I am to have a son who's so generous."

"I could've gone to Aruba with Becky Goldstein with that money!"

"Someday, son, you and I will travel to the land of milk and honey and visit your gift – your trees – the wonderful forest that bears your name. It's a *mitzvah*."

"It's a disaster!"

"May the Lord bless you and keep you, my son."

The Rabbi's Rejoinder

By H.B. Waintrup, Rabbi Emeritus
Abington, Pennsylvania

You ask whether a rabbi's son can find happiness as a tennis bum – uh – pro?

It is said in the "Sayings of our Fathers": "Who is the happy person? The one who is happy with his lot (in life)."

Son Daniel has found happiness in *tennis*. Can you imagine a Jewish parent's disappointment? Joy in *tennis*? Why not joy in becoming a rabbi?

What kind of job is it to be a tennis pro? For a Jewish son in particular? We all know that a Jewish parent's chief happiness is to have the son be a rabbi, or maybe a doctor or a lawyer. But the son a tennis pro? To be in the "Racquets"?!

How in the world will I be able to show my face in public? Not that tennis is a *shandeh* (disgrace). But look, I have said to myself, here I am − a rabbi for over fifty years. Who will carry on for me? Who will keep alive the "Waintrup" rabbinic name? Who will keep alive my three-fold ambition and excuse for entering my profession:
  (a) to be an actor,
  (b) to be a baseball player,
  (c) to be a rabbi, a teacher.

After all, I could act on the pulpit when delivering a sermon and in the process make a "hit," a home run with my congregation!

So, why couldn't son Daniel choose the pulpit as Rabbi, and thereby keep afloat my personal talent and charm?!

But here is Daniel running around like a wild animal, swinging at a ball with gusto, like a *meshugener* (crazy person).

Again I ask: What will happen to my name, my reputation? What did I do wrong? What did Dan's father and mother do to alienate their son from a glorious vocation? What was our sin? What happiness can he find as a tennis maven?

Then suddenly, quite recently actually, I have found some hope in Dan's vocation. Dan is really in a divine vocation! Dan's profession is a metaphor for living the religious life, believe it or not!

Hallelujah! With the Psalmist I lifted my rabbinic eyes to the mountaintops of purposeful living. There, I have discovered the secret of his happiness!

My help came from the Almighty, who has given me a mystic insight into the Divine Secret for Happiness. Why did I not see it before? Being "a tennis pro" is actually being a rabbi in different garments!

Yes, you've read it here. In the tennis lexicon of language there are certain esoteric words, the secret words that spell happiness for my son the "tennis knocker"! These are the words from the mystic lore of tennis: *Love, Fault, Serve, Return.* (I saw them in a book, *Tennis and the Meaning of Life,* by J. Jennings.) Daniel, our princely son, has found his happiness in these divine words, all in disguise for Judaism.

Say and think what you will, but this is the hot Kabbalistic news of the twenty-first century! Tennis really is the secret religion that can bring happiness. Its "net" value is contained in its message – How to Become "A Happy Mentsch." This news ranks high and merits our entrance into the world to come!

It was Yogi Berra who once said that baseball is ninety percent mental and the other half is physical. (Can the same thing be said for tennis?)

Certainly, the mental side of tennis is found in the "t" of tennis, which stands for the "T" of Torah (for study and learning).

Take the first key tennis word of *Love*. The Book of Deuteronomy has these words in our Prayer Book and in our Mezzuzah: "You shall Love the Lord – your God – with all your might and all your soul…" Further we are taught in Leviticus 19: "You shall love your neighbor – as yourself – I am the Lord." Hey! That's one of the great values of religion! And it's associated with tennis!

Now, how about one of the other key words of tennis? The word *Fault*. Easy, my friends. It's the "sin" factor of religion: "It is my *fault*, Lord, for I've sinned." My *fault* that the tennis ball went over the line (the boundary line of good behavior).

42

Our Yom Kippur service in the fall contains our plea to the Almighty: "Clear me, cleanse me, wash me, of all my faults so I can be reborn as a new person (a better player in life)." And this, dear friends, is part and parcel of tennis?!

Now we come to *Serve*. Serving the tennis ball, after all, keeps the game dramatic and alive. Surely, in the word *Serve*, we find religion dressed in "tennis garments." After all, how does the prophetic voice of Judaism tell us how to *serve* the Almighty?

"To do justly, to love Mercy, and to walk humbly with God."

Serving the tennis ball is the tennis way of teaching: *"Serve* God? Be a devoted and committed Jew and Human Being?!"

Finally, believe it or not, the important religious doctrine of "repentance" is part of the Tennis Divine Vision of Life.

Behold, I find it in the *Return* of the ball. Here again, *Return* finds a divine echo in Deuteronomy: *"Return* to the Lord, Repent, and God will take you back in *Love."* Tennis again! Love!

No escaping from tennis, it has all the litany of religion: *Love, Serve* (God), watch out for your *Faults* (your sins), repent – *Return* – the Ball of Life properly and you'll be a winner!

Find happiness, as Daniel, the child wonder of our lives, has found it, in tennis, dear friends.

Long ago, Father Abraham was told to instruct his children in the Good Way of Life, Justice, and Mercy. Is it possible that Father Abraham also intended to instruct his children in the proper "match" points for a Good Marriage? For a Good Life?

May our son, Daniel, continue to find happiness as a tennis pro. Like Father Abraham, may he instruct many students to find happiness as has he.

In the end, how can I not be happy that my son is a tennis pro? After all, remember, dear friends, in the Bible, Joseph served in Pharaoh's court!

Amen!

Dear Mr. Country Club Tennis Pro,

Have you ever given your father a tennis lesson? If you have, what was it like teaching him?

Signed,
Rose Rosenberg

Dear Rose,

I did give my father a lesson once, and I found that I had to communicate a little differently than I would if I were teaching a less religiously inclined individual. Instead of saying (as I would have if I were teaching one of my regular students), "Keep your eyes high and reach up if you want to hit those overheads well," I found the phrasing had to be a little different when teaching my father the same shot: "Thou shalt reach up and lift up thine eyes toward the Lord your God, Rabbi, if you want to hit those overheads well!"

Waintrup's Rules for Winning
The Serve

Learning to serve is all about repetition. It's all about developing the "circle of power," as it used to be called. It's all about developing a fluid, relaxed overhand throwing motion. It's all about taking your racquet back, bending your elbow, feeling the slow to fast motion of your racquet accelerating through the "back scratch" position, hitting up and out through a contact point that's (hopefully) to the right and in front of your body (if you're right-handed).

Hitting an effective serve can be a real challenge if you don't have a certain level of coordination, but it's not difficult to work on and improve — if you know what the hell to work on! "If you can throw a ball overhand, you can serve," I tell my students over and over and over again. Problem is, the majority of the individuals I work with have never learned how to throw a ball correctly, so they always had trouble serving effectively. As one of my most elegant country club students once put it, "The only thing I've ever thrown is a dinner party!"

It's not uncommon for me to take the first half of a lesson and focus on the serve. We work on the mechanics of throwing — the mechanics of simply taking a ball, raising your throwing/serving arm, bending your elbow and turning your shoulder, and releasing the ball in a nice, relaxed, fluid manner. The great

45

thing about this motion is that it's something you can practice on your own. You don't need to pay a tennis pro $65 an hour to watch you serve once you understand the motion and the basic idea behind the shot. (I know, I know — hard to believe, but I have actually said that to many of my students!)

"How do you think I learned to serve?" I ask my students. "As a high school student, I would take a bucket of balls, go out on a tennis court, and work on getting comfortable with the motion."

"But I can never find a court to play on," they tell me. If you can't find a court, find a wall, stand fifteen to twenty feet away (you don't need a lot of balls for this drill), and work on understanding the way your body moves when you are doing this important motion. "If you can't find a wall," I continue, "go out with your spouse or your kids and play catch." ("Don't worry, you can go in the backyard, Mrs. Lebowitz. No one will see!")

Learning to serve is all about the repetition. You may never serve like Andy Roddick or Serena Williams, but if you take the time to practice this motion, if you put your time in on the practice court (or in the backyard!) you will improve one of the most important shots in the game. (See photograph #7, pg. 50.)

Dear Mr. Country Club
Tennis Pro,

So what if your father's a
rabbi and you teach ten-
nis for a living? What's so
great? What's so unique
about that?

Signed,
Unimpressed

Dear Unimpressed,

How many tennis pros do
you know who can teach a
topspin forehand and last
week's Torah portion in the
same lesson?

Dear Mr. Country Club Tennis Pro,

Is it really true that you got the job
here at the club because your father
is a rabbi?

Signed,
Mrs. Lipshitz

Dear Mrs. Lipshitz,

While I'd like to think that I
got the job based on my own
merits, the predominantly
Jewish hiring committee
may have been somewhat
influenced by the presence of
my father behind me during
the entire interview singing,
"I Had a Little Dreidel."

Dear Mr. Country Club Tennis Pro,

When are you going to get a real job, you schmendrick? Look at you, running around all day, flirting with women, perspiring, and getting overheated. It's a wonder you don't catch your death of cold! Is this any way for a nice, Jewish boy from Philadelphia to make a living?

Signed,
Someone Who Cares

Dear Mother,

We've already discussed this – and I'm not going to graduate school!

48

#5.

"Even before I graduated from high
school, I had a thing for older women."

#6.

Even though the Rabbi was quite
the baseball player, he decided to
make his "hit" from the pulpit.

Dan tries to get up to the ball
for his famous Viagra serve!

Dan's father reacts to his son telling him he
wants to become a tennis pro.

3. Getting Paid to Play – What a Way to Make a Living

Dear Mr. Country Club Tennis Pro,

I know you're an unbelievably steady player. Isn't it true in college that they use to call you "The Human Wall"?

Signed,
Mel Moskowitz

Dear Mel,

Actually, it's true. I was such a consistent player during my collegiate days that my teammates gave me that nickname. Of course, being a rabbi's son teaching at a Jewish country club, it's been changed to "The Wailing Wall"!

Up Against "The Wall"

In truth, tennis was absolutely the last sport I ever thought that I'd end up playing and, ultimately, having a career in. I knew nothing about the game growing up, about its history or its many great players and personalities.

I wanted to be a baseball player like my old man. Like the Rabbi, I was a good fielder, but I could never learn to hit a curve ball. I also loved football and dreamed of being a wide receiver in the NFL. But as I got older, and my opponents got bigger and tougher, the physical punishment that went with catching a pass over the middle was not something I really wanted to deal with. For a long time I thought basketball would be my game. I was quick and deadly accurate from anywhere on the court. But at 5 feet 10 inches, my lack of size was a major obstacle.

By process of elimination, that left tennis. You didn't have to be the biggest kid on the block, or the strongest guy in the world to excel on a tennis court. If you had good hand-eye coordination and reaction skills, were mentally tough, and could run all day, you could give anybody a match. I really knew I was on to something when, after only two lessons and a couple of weeks of practice, I started regularly beating guys who had been playing for a couple of years.

My game really started to develop my freshman year in high school. The truth was that I had nothing better to do with my spare time. All the girls who had loved me the year before were now enamored with the sophomores and juniors (and their cars!). It was definitely a lonely time for the Rabbi's son. Out of sheer boredom, I picked up a wooden, Stan Smith-autographed tennis racquet (talk about showing your age!), and a can of balls, went down to the local public courts, and started hitting against the wall. (For a picture of Dan's wall see photograph #20, pg. 190.)

I spent a lot of hours against that wall. You'd be surprised how steady and consistent you can get hitting against a backboard for hours and hours and hours. My strokes were unorthodox, but I became very consistent. Like a wall, "The Human Wall," as my tennis buddies and opponents started to call me (a name that would stick with me for my entire high school, collegiate, and teaching pro career).

53

As I improved, I thought that I might try out for the high school team my junior year. I didn't make it, and I was livid. I was certain that I was better than the majority of players who had tried out.

"The coach must be anti-Semitic," I bitterly told my friends.

"That's not likely," they assured me, "since he's an orthodox Jew!"

Accepting the fact that maybe I wasn't good enough, I used this setback in a positive way, working hard the following year on my game, and making the team my senior year. I was undefeated as a senior, and the only member of our school team to win a match against our hated rivals in the season-ending championships.

I dreamed of playing at the collegiate level, but few people gave me much of a chance. As has been a recurring pattern in my life, I proved everyone wrong. I made the Temple University varsity squad as a freshman and played for three seasons. My junior year was spent in Jerusalem, where I played for Hebrew University's tennis team. We had a great team at Temple in the '70s, a great group of guys from all over the world. We were East Coast Conference Champions for three years. And – talk about an interesting collection of personalities – this team could have had a starring role in *Animal House*. In the words of the immortal Steve Martin, "We were a bunch of wild and crazy guys!" Few of us ever saw a party we didn't want to participate in, or a blonde we didn't want to chase after. Looking back, it's a miracle we played as well as we did.

I'll always remember my good friend and teammate telling me, after we had partied all night and he had lost his match the following day against an opponent from the highly ranked team we were playing, "I felt good during the match. I just kept falling down!"

I loved the game and I enjoyed the competition, but playing tennis had other benefits as well. It was a great way to meet women and an easy way to make money. Like most of the collegiate tennis players I knew, I started teaching in college during the summers to make a few extra dollars. I certainly never imagined that it would turn into a career.

I truly thought I was going to make the world tour. I wanted to emulate my idols. I wanted to be like Jimmy Connors and Bjorn Borg. At twenty-three, I dreamed of playing the tour, but it was not to be.

The first moment I became acutely aware that I wouldn't be playing tennis with players named Connors and Borg, but teaching tennis to players named Goldstein and Berkawitz, occurred during a tournament I was playing in during the summer of 1981. During this time, after the successful collegiate career I had had, I was absolutely certain that I was good enough to hold my own on a tennis court with anyone. However, during a match in the third round of the New England Men's Singles Championships, I came to the painful realization that maybe I didn't quite have what it takes to play with the big boys.

55

The match I'm referring to put me up against a player named Michael Leach, an individual who had played for the University of Michigan team. At that time, Mr. Leach had played a number of players ranked in the Top 100 in the world and played them very competitively. I knew that this match would really tell me if I had the ability to compete with someone who was widely regarded as having world-class ability.

During the warm-up I kept waiting to see this huge serve everyone had been talking about, but, strangely enough, it just didn't seem that powerful to me. "Maybe everyone has just been exaggerating about how great this guy was," I thought to myself. Unfortunately, I was soon to find out the hard way that my opponent was only hitting his practice serves at a fraction of their normal speed!

I made this discovery in a nanosecond. On the first point of our match, Mr. Leach hit his first serve so powerfully and so swiftly that the only thing I saw was the mark the ball left on the clay court that we were playing on.

"Gee," I thought to myself, "he must have hit that one 110, maybe 120 mph. This is going to be great fun!"

I was just trying to humor myself before the devastation, destruction, and humiliation this man was about to inflict on me and my tennis game. Needless to say, being barely able to see, let alone return, your opponent's serve is not only a disheartening experience, but an intimidating one as well.

After the first game, in which I was cleanly aced on four straight serves, my main goals were to:
- Get off the court without being injured or maimed by one of Mr. Leach's incredible deliveries,
- See if I could win one game,
- Finish the match as quickly as possible so no one would see how outclassed I was.

I failed miserably on all three counts! The match may have been one of the quickest and most lopsided in New England tournament history. Lucky for me, I invited all my friends and relatives to watch the match and share in this wonderful experience. As my opponent blazed one last return past my outstretched racquet, I thought to myself, "I wonder if I still have that business school application?"

As I crawled to the net to congratulate my conqueror, the course of my tennis career changed forever.

My opponent couldn't have been nicer. "Nice match, you'll get me next time."

"Right," I said. "Terrific match, I really pushed you hard, almost got you to take those warm-ups off… By the way, do you know any clubs in the area that are looking for a good teaching pro?" (See photograph #10, pg. 74.)

My favorite player growing up was Vitas Gerulaitis. I dreamed I would party all night like he did (preferably at Studio 54) and play tennis all day. I wanted to disco 'til dawn with some beautiful fashion model (Cheryl Tiegs!) and then win the tournament the next day in Paris or London or LA. Unfortunately, I wasn't as good as Vitas Gerulaitis, and I didn't have the money or the financial backing to try and play the world tour. I had to get a job when I got out of college and pay the rent. Teaching tennis was the easiest way for me to make a living.

57

Dear Mr. Country Club Tennis Pro,

I've always wondered how in the world you guys can have so much patience when you teach. I mean, some of the people you have to work with are really terrible. How in the world do you keep from getting bored?

Signed,
Debby Goldberg

Dear Debby,

You'd be amazed how much patience you can have when you're getting paid.

Dan Gets a Paying Gig

They say timing is everything in life. This was certainly the case when I applied for the tennis teaching job at the country club. I had a number of distinct advantages over the other candidates. The first of these was the fact that the hiring committee was looking for a pro with a teaching style that was a little more positive than their former employee. They were looking for an individual who understood that the majority of the students he or she was going to work with did not have the talent, time, or desire to become world class players. They were looking for a teaching professional who didn't tell his or her pupils how "horrible" they were; they were looking for someone who would tell them how "wonderful" they were.

They were looking for a pro like Dan Waintrup.

Probably the most important factor in my favor when I applied for the country club teaching job was that, for some reason, I didn't seem to have a lot of competition for it. I never really found out why more tennis pros didn't apply for what was one of the most lucrative teaching jobs in New England. What I did find out after I got the job was that the hiring committee had a pretty easy choice. After narrowing their search down to me and another pro, my main competitor told them in his last interview: "I think I'd do a good job here. Some of my best friends are Jews. My family doesn't like 'em much, but I can get along with them if I have to."

God bless those anti-Semites!

Dear Mr. Country Club Tennis Pro,

I've taken tennis lessons from many different pros all over the world. I was just wondering – is there any way you can tell if you're taking a lesson from a Jewish teaching professional?

Signed,
Gerry Goldfarb

60

Dear Gerry,

The real key here is to listen to the pro's instruction.

Non-Jewish Instruction	Jewish Instruction
"Bend your knees."	"Bend your knees, bubby."
"You call that an overhand?"	"Oy vey, you call that an overhand?"
"Don't worry, you can pay me next week."	"Pay me now or I'll sue!"

Dear Mr. Country Club Tennis Pro,

All my friends have been telling me that most country club tennis teaching professionals are just a big bunch of selfish, greedy, money-hungry individuals who care nothing about the game of tennis and only about themselves. How would you respond to such a charge?

Signed,
Patricia

61

Dear Patricia,

Well, as you can probably imagine, I'm shocked by such an allegation! My love for the game is exceeded only by my love for the people I have the privilege to work with. Anyone who knows me is acutely aware that I would teach tennis for free. Anytime you'd like to come down to the club, meet me, maybe play a little tennis, and see how much I enjoy the game and how unimportant the monetary aspect of tennis teaching is for me, right now, I'm just sixty-three cents a minute! Come on down!

Dear Mr. Country Club Tennis Pro,

Do you ever accept other forms of payment besides money for your lessons?

Signed,
Mordecai

Dear Mordecai,

Actually, I did try it once. One of my students was a dentist, and he wanted to trade tennis lessons for dental work. What seemed like a good idea at the time, however, turned out to be a nightmare. I gave him a few lessons, at $65 an hour, and went to him because I needed a new filling. Unfortunately, when I saw his bill I realized I had made a slight miscalculation in judgment. I owed him $2,500, or forty tennis lessons! It took me eight months to pay him back!

Dear Mr. Country Club Tennis Pro,

I can't believe I just bought another racquet from your pro shop! God! That must be four or five this year alone! I was just wondering, what's the most number of racquets that you ever sold to one student?

Signed,
Rachel

Dear Rachel,

Well, Rachel, you can rest assured that you're not close to the record for racquets purchased by a student in a twelve-month period. I had this sucker – uh – student once with an extremely violent temper. In truth, I was scared to death to be on the court with him. He'd insist on taking playing lessons with me, and every time he'd make a mistake (which would usually be before me, because you know, bubby, I don't miss – I'm the pro, "The Human Ball Machine," "The Human Wall," etc...), he'd smash his frame on the court in disgust. After the tenth or eleventh mistake, my student would usually have one or two very large cracks in the frame of his racquet.

I'd say, "You know, Joel, looks like that frame isn't going to make it, but fortunately for you, I just got in that new Wilson racquet that everybody's talking about."

Joel, being insanely wealthy, would say, "Great, string it up and I'll see you next week."

Truth be told, I sold this guy fifteen frames in a six-month period! (God, I loved that man!) Unfortunately for me, however, and my growing collection of Rolex watches, my student did something that I think I may never forgive him for – he started going to anger management classes!

Damn those therapists.

Dear Mr. Country Club Tennis Pro,

I know you've already explained in your newsletter how one knows if he or she is taking a lesson from a Jewish tennis pro, but I was just wondering, how would one know if he or she was watching a match between two Jewish tennis pros?

Signed,
Terry Titlebaum

64

Dear Terry,

Actually, it's very simple. While non-Jewish tennis professionals keep score among themselves during a match, Jewish pros use an accountant!

Often, I've found that I have to be aggressive in my pursuit of lessons here at the country club!

Waintrup's Rules for Winning
Volley

If you ever want to be a truly advanced player in tennis, you have to learn how to volley. You have to learn the form of the shot that will allow you to come to net and finish off a point. To execute the shot, grip the racquet firmly and lock your wrist; meet the ball in front of your body with a short, solid, punching motion. What grip to use? There is some room for individual interpretation here.

While you see many beginner and intermediate players using an eastern forehand grip for their forehand volley, more advanced players utilize the continental grip. For the backhand volley, one or two hands can be used, depending on:

- Personal preference,
- Skill and coordination level,
- And often, the particular tennis pro who's teaching the shot.

Sometimes when students are having difficulty with this shot, I find it useful to give them visual cues.

"Come on, Mr. Levine! You've got to give me some aggression here! You're not punching, bubby. You know that guy from the SEC? Yeah, the jerk that wants to put you in jail – think of the ball as his face. That's it! Now you got it! Right between the eyes! Great volley that time!"

66

The most important element of the shot? Think of your hand, wrist, arm, racquet, and shoulder as one unit. Think of this one, solid, punching unit moving forward to hit the ball. Think of it as a backboard – your backboard. Practice learning the feeling of controlling the ball. Controlling the volley off your backboard. Start with slow balls and work your way up to fast balls. When you practice the shot, work on volleying from different parts of the court and on balls that you have to hit at different heights and contact points.

Once you've mastered the volley form, once you understand this feeling of "oneness," as I like to call it, you will realize that when you come to net, you must be keenly aware of the height of the ball when you make contact. Logically, the lower the contact point, the more open the racquet face; the higher the contact point, the more vertical. Developing an awareness of the height of the ball when you're volleying, the speed of the ball when it's coming at you, and where you are on the tennis court when you make contact, are extremely important aspects of the shot that can only be learned through hours of practice, drilling, and match play.

In my mind, understanding the volley technique and its utilization at net is not the only important aspect of volleying. Being the ultimate pusher, "The Human Wall" as I was so affectionately named by my college teammates, the real value of the volley for me was being able to utilize this technique from anywhere on the court, especially from "no man's land" (that dreaded area behind the service line) and the baseline. The ability to "block" back the overheads, volleys, and offensive groundstrokes of opposing players gave me the chance to stay in the rally and, more often than not, win the point from an increasingly frustrated and overanxious opponent.

One of the most important principles I have tried to get across to my students over the years, and one that every player needs to remember, is that you win matches by being consistent, you win matches by out-steadying your opponent, you win matches by letting your opponent make a mistake. Being able to "volley" back your opponent's shots and giving him or her one more chance to "choke" is an extremely important aspect of winning tennis, and one that often gets overlooked by players at every skill level.

Learning the technique of the volley is extremely important if you're ever going to be an advanced tennis player. While working with a pro is the best way to master it, it's not the only way. Take out a ball machine and practice with it. Find a hitting wall and see how many times you can volley the ball in the air. Go out with a friend and work on volleying the ball - see how many times you can do it in a row. Understanding the volley form is vital if you want to keep improving as a player. In my own experience, learning how to volley early on as a player allowed me to get out on a court with better players; they knew I could consistently block back their shots and give them a workout, so they agreed to play with me, helping me improve my game.

68

Practice the form. Practice learning the feeling of controlling the shots off "your backboard." Practice punching the ball aggressively. And, if you need to give yourself a visual image like our friend Morty Levine, so be it. In my own experience, I really started to volley the ball more aggressively and effectively during my divorce - "You want the house and the car?!"

The Ex-Wife Begs to Differ

Where in the world did you come up with the title for this chapter? "Getting Paid to Play - What a Way to Make A Living" - what living? You call that a living? If you were truly making a living during our marriage, I don't think you would have been driving that beat-up, ten-year-old Datsun of yours. You know, the one with

140,000 miles on it? The one where you had to kick the passenger side door in just to close it? The one that smelled so bad (especially every summer after sitting in the sun all day) from all the egg McMuffins, coffees, and apple danishes you'd stuff your face with every morning on the way to the club?

The playing part of your title is very accurate – you played all right! During the day I could maybe have understood it, but how did you play tennis all night?

Why couldn't you ever get a real job? My cousin said he could get you a job at the kosher butcher. Why couldn't you just be a regular person? What was so wrong with that? Why were you trying to have fun all the time? Real people don't have fun; real people don't talk loud like you and try to make dumb jokes all the time. What was so special about you that you think you should be happy? Real people don't hang out at country clubs all day, play tennis with rich guys, and flirt with their wives. What a *shmendrick!*

69

How much are you earning from this stupid book anyway? Did you get a big advance like Hillary Clinton? Nobody is interested in your story! Have you negotiated the movie rights?

You'll be hearing from my lawyer!

"My uncle always described an unforced error as his first marriage."

                                        – Bud Collins

Dear Mr. Country Club Tennis Pro,

I know that the majority of your income here at the country club is derived from the lessons you give and the merchandise you sell in your pro shop. I was just wondering, however, if you've discovered other ways to generate revenue for yourself?

Signed,
Daniel

Dear Daniel,

My favorite method of making more money here at the country club is when I run those mixed doubles round-robins and force the husbands and wives to play together for the entire event. At the tournament's conclusion, after the once-happy couples are finished screaming expletives at each other and trying for outright decapitation or dismemberment. I calmly pull one of the husbands or wives aside and say, "You know, relationships are always tough. Sometimes it takes a little tennis to see what people are really like. Here, take this card; it's the number of my cousin, Morris. Many think he's the best divorce attorney in the state."

(Can you say "referral fee?")

"Talk to any marriage counselor and you'll learn that mixed doubles has caused more divorces than mothers-in-law."

– Bud Collins

Dear Mr. Country Club Tennis Pro,

I know that you've run many tournaments in your career here at the country club. I was just wondering, what's the strangest experience you've ever had as a tournament chairman?

Signed,
Donald Dell

Dear Donald,

The strangest experience I've ever had was the time a few years back when I was running a men's 45 and Over tournament and handing out the starting times to all the participants. As it turned out, one of the players appeared to have his priorities a little screwed up.

"Hello, yes! I'm trying to reach Dave Goldberg."

"Yes, I'm Dave Goldberg."

cont.

"I just wanted to give you your starting time for the men's championships coming up at the club this weekend."

"Great. When's my first round?"

"We have you playing at 10:30 Saturday morning, okay, sir?"

"Gee, that might be a problem. You know, I'm a surgeon and I have an operation in the morning. You know what, don't worry about it. I'll be there. I'm sure I'll be able to finish the procedure in time."

"Look, maybe I could give you a later starting time. We are talking about surgery, right, Doctor?"

"Listen, don't worry about it. I'll rush through it. It's not a big deal. This tournament is really important to me. Who am I playing?"

"Jesus! Don't rush through the operation! I'd be happy to give you a later starting time!"

"Is it Sandy Mendelson? I know I'm playing Sandy Mendelson. That son of a bitch took me in three sets last weekend. He gave me the worst line calls."

cont.

"Look, Dr. Goldberg. Think of your patient! You can play later on Saturday for god-sakes!"

"Don't worry about the goddamn operation! I can do it with my eyes closed. Besides, you should see this brand new Wilson racquet I just got; I'm killing my forehand right now!"

"I don't want you killing anything. That's why I want to give you a later starting time!"

"Would you forget the operation, please? Whatever happens happens. And besides, I'm feeling great about my game right now. I know this is going to be my tournament!"

73

"I think you're crazy! God help your patient!"

"God help my opponent. I'll see you in the winner's circle, bubby!"

"I have a feeling I'll be seeing you, not only on court, doctor, but in court as well!"

Let the record reflect, if anything happens, it's not my fault!

#9.

Jay O'Brien

"Even after playing the game for thirty-five years, it's evident from this picture that I am still aware of one of the most important aspects of playing well on a tennis court, keeping your head down through contact."

74

#10.

"The Wall" contemplates throwing himself in front of a moving automobile after his resounding defeat in the third round of the New England Men's Singles Championships.

"Looking back at the photo of my mother
and me before I walked down the aisle for
the first time, I can't help thinking – If I
only knew now what I didn't know then."

4. Country Club Tennis Instruction for Dummies

Dear Mr. Country Club Tennis Pro,

I love taking lessons with you, but I'm get incredibly frustrated because I can't always understand what you're really trying to say to me. Am I an idiot or have some of your other students mentioned having the same problem?

Signed,
Lauren Stein

Dear Lauren,

It's not your fault. At times some of my students have said to me that I can be a little vague. As a teaching pro, I should be able to communicate clearly enough so that anyone can comprehend what I'm trying to say. Hopefully, the chart below will help you understand me a little better.

When the country club pro says:	He really means:
"You've got a million-dollar forehand."	"It's going to cost you a million dollars to have a good forehand."
"You really have a lot of potential."	"Your game is pathetic, but if you take three lessons a week for the next five years, there's an outside chance that someday you'll be able to have a rally with someone!"
"You're really a deceptive player."	"You have no idea where the ball is going when you hit it."
"There appears to be a few things we can work on in your game."	"There's a very good chance you won't be appearing on the cover of *Tennis Magazine* anytime soon!"

cont.

"Great shot! Didn't miss by much that time."

"Your shot was actually three to five feet too long."

"I saw you practicing the other day, and I think you and I are going to be good friends!"

"Leave the Visa Gold at the front desk!"

"If you play well, I'm your pro. If you play poorly, we've never met!"

Self-explanatory.

79

It's a Tough Job, but Somebody's Got To Do It!

If you ever get a job teaching at a big, prestigious country club, there are a number of important rules that you must remember if you are to succeed. The most important of these is the realization that the majority of your new students are extremely wealthy individuals. Because of this fact, the ability to work on improving their tennis games will often be adversely affected by the almost limitless number of recreational choices that are available to them.

Consequently, the country club tennis pro must learn not to get upset if a student decides that jetting down to the

Caribbean for some scuba diving sounds a little more exciting than taking out a bucket of balls and working on his or her slice serve. In another of my own experiences, how could I have been disappointed when my women's team had to default on the day of the league championship match? Hey, it wasn't their fault – that was the week they had all decided to go to the spa!

The second important rule that you must remember when you start working at a country club is the understanding that your teaching will be a little different than in the past. Give your students what they want, not what you think they want. As the pro, you must realize that the majority of the individuals with whom you're now working aren't in training to travel the world professional tour. They don't have to; they own the companies and banks that sponsor it!

Because of this important fact, you must never force anyone at a country club to do anything they don't want to do. I had a tennis pro friend who insisted on ignoring this important idea, forcing his country club students to start their lessons off with sit-ups and wind sprints. Last we heard, he was fixing pipelines in Iraq! In light of this important concept, I've compiled a few helpful instructional phrases to aid the country club pro in the teaching of his new students.

REGULAR INSTRUCTION	COUNTRY CLUB INSTRUCTION
"Bend your knees."	"Bend your knees, if you don't mind."
"Swing low to high on your groundstrokes."	"Swing low to high on your groundstrokes, if that would be okay with you."
"Transfer your weight into the shot."	"Transfer what little weight you have into the shot." (For women students.)

The third important principle you must follow if you are to succeed as a country club tennis pro is the development of the ability to stretch the truth. (Okay, okay – you've got to lie a little bit; you may recall this is a particular skill of mine discovered at an early age.) As the pro, it's your job to convince every student at your club that they have the potential to be a better player. When Mrs. Lebowitz, who hasn't hit a backhand in the court since the summer of '75, comes up to you for the twenty-third time that week and asks you if you honestly feel that she's improving the shot that she's spent $5,000 on and that once killed a low-flying bird, you must say, "Absolutely, darling!"

Another significant rule that must be strictly followed if the country club pro is to be successful: stay cool under pressure. You must have an innate sense of how to deal with the misunderstandings and hassles that often occur in the pro's day-to-day life. For example, recently I was

81

hurrying to a lesson at my country club when a member suddenly accosted me and demanded to know where his tennis racquet was that I was supposed to have strung for him two weeks ago. Having no idea what he was talking about, or even who the man was, the situation called for some creative thinking.

"Gee, I'm sorry, sir, the racquet was going to be dropped off last Friday but... The stringer's car was hit by a bus, terrible accident, nylon and gut string all over the place. But I'm sure I could get it to you by tomorrow if that wouldn't be too much of an inconvenience."

The country club tennis pro must always look like he or she is in complete control of the situation.

Another important rule you must follow if you are to succeed as a country club tennis pro is the realization that you must possess or develop good acting skills. Having the ability to make your student look good without him or her actually knowing it is very important and, potentially, very profitable. For example, if you were giving a playing lesson to one of your wealthy clients, an individual who might be considering a career for you in his highly successful company, or paying you to play with him five times a week, beating him 6 - 0, 6 - 0 would be the wrong thing to do. Allowing him to win a few points or games now and then and grunting like the immortal Jimmy Connors as you blow that forehand down the line (that you normally wouldn't miss unless you were blind drunk or blindfolded) is a great way of making your student look good and come back for more.

Another equally important key to succeeding as a country club tennis professional is the establishment of a pro shop that sells the most expensive tennis clothing and equipment on the market. Naturally, this means the pro must be dressed in these expensive clothes and using this highly priced equipment. Today, country club teaching professionals all over the world are extremely fortunate that modern technology has allowed for the design of extremely powerful tennis racquets that require little form or effort to achieve success. Your students are virtually guaranteed to put their shots in play with this new equipment. At my club, the introduction of these powerful wide-body racquets was as important to many of my students in their lives as a sale at Armani.

We affectionately called the Wilson Widebody frame introduced on the market several years ago as the "first Jewish tennis racquet." The first tennis racquet specifically designed for the Jewish American Princess – no effort needed to succeed! I sold sixty frames the first week they came on the market. (God, I love this country!) Another key to my pro shop's success, and the acquisition of my new Lamborghini, was convincing my clients to buy one of these extraordinarily powerful frames for each of their houses. Thus, one of my best clients, Libby Lipshitz, bought one for the mansion in Manchester, for the villa in St. Tropez, and for the condo in Palm Beach! Since the selling of tennis racquets is probably the most important activity that the country club pro can do to ensure his financial success, I've listed a few phrases that can help convince your student that the frame you're having him or her try out and, of course, the one that

83

the pro also uses and makes the most money on, is the right one for him or her.

Phrases that sell:
(Say these with feeling; think Al Pacino in *Dog Day Afternoon.*)

"Look, I don't care if you shell out the money or not, but I can't believe how much better you're playing with that frame!"

"Boy, are you pounding those volleys today!"

"You don't have to buy it, but if you want my professional opinion, it seems to fit your game perfectly!"

"I don't think I've ever seen you hit with better depth and control!"

"Playing you now – it's like playing against Agassi!"

"You know, it doesn't look good when the student is hitting the ball harder than the pro!"

"Now I know what it's like to try and return a serve like Roddick's!"

"Can you teach me to hit with that kind of power?! I've created a monster!"

Another important principle you must follow if you are to succeed as a country club tennis pro is knowing how to communicate with your new clientele. You need to be able to talk to your wealthy students about things they can relate to. Below I've listed a number of excellent conversation starters that every country club pro should find invaluable.

"How was the trip to Paris?"

"How's the South Beach diet going?"

"How's your son/daughter enjoying the new private school?"

"How was the food at the opera gala?"

85

"I saw you on the first tee; you're hitting your drives a ton!"

"I saw you at the reception. I love the new outfit! Is it Prada?"

"How did the market open today?"

HOW LONG DO YOU THINK THIS ANGER TOWARDS YOUR MOTHER HAS AFFECTED YOUR TOPSPIN FOREHAND?

The successful country club teaching professional must be able to work with his clientele in more ways than teaching them how to hit their groundstrokes

86

The last and probably most important rule that must be adhered to if you are to thrive and prosper as a country club tennis teaching professional is having or developing a sense of humor. If you can keep your students laughing at their mistakes and learning from them, they have a better chance of improving as players, and you have a better chance of seeing them in between trips to the Caribbean. As I told one of my students recently after he was continually having trouble executing a high, deep, defensive lob, "Hey, don't worry about it. I know a lot of guys who have trouble getting it up!"

Here are a few more phrases that a country club pro might be able to use to keep his or her students from getting too depressed after they repeatedly make a specific error during a lesson:

When you're rallying with your student in the singles court, and he or she continually hits the ball wide – in the doubles alley: "You know, Myron, you're probably one of the most natural doubles players I've ever seen!"

When your student continually hits the ball long or over the back fence: "Hey, what's thirty feet out when you really think about it?"

When your student makes every possible mistake he or she could make on a particular shot; too wristy, swinging too hard, wrong grip: "Mrs. Lebowitz, it's amazing how many things you did wrong on that shot!"

When your student keeps mishitting his or her shots, consistently having the ball strike the frame and shaft of his or her racquet, rarely the strings: "You know, it's unbelievable how many different parts of the racquet you use when you play!"

87

When your student swings at the ball and misses completely: "You may have missed the ball by two feet, but your form was perfect!"

When your student hits a volley onto Court Two, and you're giving him or her a lesson on Court One: "Great angle that time!"

The Definitive List of Country Club Tennis Drills

1. The "FBI" Drill

Invented at one of the first country clubs many years ago, "FBI" is an extremely important drill for any country club pro to utilize, since in a game or drill your new students will rarely be capable of getting the "[F]irst [B]all [I]n" (or any other shot they attempt, for that matter).

2. The "Hit and Don't Move" Drill

The traditional "Hit and Move" drill isn't applicable at a country club for obvious reasons, but there are variations that can be employed by the pro. "Hit and Stand," or "Hit and Don't Move," as it's most commonly known, is one of the truly necessary drills that must exist in every country club professional's repertoire. The goal here is to encourage success for your students by hitting or feeding the ball at a nice slow speed right at them, waist high, and with no spin. The key to the drill's success depends on the pro's ability to be accurate with his placement of the ball so that his student never has to move more than one step in either direction (and, God forbid, break a sweat!).

3. The "Hit and Talk" Drill

Self-explanatory. A very popular drill used primarily in women's clinics.

4. The "Hit and Complain" Drill

The country club pro should be prepared for many variations of this drill. At most Jewish country clubs, the drill may be better known by the name "Hit and *Kvetch*."

5. The "Hit and Shop" Drill

Probably the most popular drill at any country club among your female clientele.

6. The "Hit and Hug" Drill

A drill designed primarily for the better-looking women at your club.

7. The "Hit and Don't Hug" Drill

A drill designed for the sisters and relatives of the better-looking women at your club.

8. The "Hit and Relax" Drill

The successful country club teaching pro must never overwork his new clientele. ("Forehand, backhand, two minute rest... Forehand, backhand, two minute rest...")

89

9. The "Water Break"

The most important country club tennis drill.

10. The "Let's Come Back to that Later" Drill

The country club teaching professional realizes during a lesson that his or her student hasn't the time, desire, or ability to learn (or work on learning) a particular shot, but promises to come back and work on it "later." (Translation: "Not in this lifetime.")

11. The "What Would You Like to Work on Today, Sir?" Drill

An extremely important drill for the country club pro who's just starting out. In the drill, the pro is acutely aware of the fact that many of his new clients are extremely rich and powerful individuals, and that in the lesson, if he doesn't work on what they want, the pro's next hour of instruction has a good chance of taking place at the public courts down on 168th street!

12. The "Crawl to the Ball" Drill

If the country club tennis pro wishes to be successful, it's imperative that he or she starts taking advantage of the extreme wealth of his or her new clientele as soon as possible. At my club it isn't uncommon to see me teaching one- or two-year-old infants. For those parents who might question the wisdom of teaching tennis to children so young, the country club pro need only say, "Hey, Jimmy Connors was only three years old when he first picked up a racquet, and today he's worth over $50 million!" (Believe me, that's a statement that they'll be able to relate to.) Another great drill for this age group: "Hit and Go Smelly." (See photograph #13, pg. 131.)

13. The "Hit the Pro" Drill, or as it's commonly known, "Maim that Pro – Junior Version"

An extremely popular drill at any country club, designed specifically for younger players. After being holed up in private school all day, many country club juniors will have an enormous amount of energy that needs to be released while their mothers go shopping. In the drill, the pro feeds forehands and backhands to his or her students and awards monetary prizes if they can successfully hit different parts of the pro's anatomy with their groundstrokes (for example: one dollar for an arm, two dollars for a leg…). Protective gear may be necessary for the tennis teacher as many country club juniors will often try for outright decapitation, or smashing a Pro Penn at one of the pro's own Pro Penns!

The country club tennis pro during one of his junior player's favorite drills - 'Hit the Pro'

91

13a. The "Hit the Pro - Junior Version," also known as "Aim for the Pickle"

The country club tennis professional may want to enhance the target practice he gives his junior students in "Hit the Pro" by having them aim for one specific part of the pro's body. In "Aim for the Pickle," or as it's commonly known at most Jewish country clubs, "Aim for the Kosher Dill Pickle," the tennis pro is getting his students to improve their game by having them drive their forehands and backhands at the pro's nose, which, in my case, and for most Jewish tennis teaching professionals, resembles a pickle or large vegetable.

13b. The "Hit the Pro – Adult Male Version," also known as "Mash the *Matzah* Ball" (the title of this drill can be adjusted for non-Jewish tennis teaching professionals)

An extremely important drill for your adult male clientele, especially when they've had a bad day at the office. Your student will need to release all his anger for not receiving that desperately needed business loan. In the drill itself, the country club professional feeds nice, easy forehands (or whatever stroke can be hit hardest) to his student so that he can really pound out his frustrations on the ball. As he swings as hard as he can, you might have him scream out, "Take that Bank of America!" In view of the often therapeutic value of this drill, country club pros should not be afraid to charge double or triple their normal hourly rate.

13c. The "Hit the Pro – Adult Female Version," favorite Jewish country club variation – "Pulverize the Potato Latke"

Similar drill for your adult female clientele, who have just as many problems and the need to release just as many tensions as their male counterparts (they can't find the au pair they want, they're upset that their vacation plans this month are in the Virgin Islands instead of Aruba…). As in the junior and adult male versions of the drill, your female students get to work on the accuracy of their forehand and backhand groundstrokes by attempting to hit various parts of the pro's anatomy. The country club tennis pro can use his creativity to make the drill fun and interesting. For example, at the country club, my girls really started to enjoy the drill when they realized that if they were successful in hitting me with a tennis ball they would receive a gift certificate towards their very next Botox or liposuction appointment!

14. The "Make the Country Club Tennis Pro Wish He Had Gone to Law School" Drill

A very popular drill at any country club, primarily among your more advanced players, former collegiate stars, and one-time teaching professionals who have now moved on to a "real job" in the family business. In the drill, these players book time with the country club pro either at 6 a.m., when they know the pro has the coordination of a pregnant water buffalo, or after he's worked all day and is completely exhausted. They demand to play sets and enjoy watching a typically talented tennis player stumble for easy shots, miss balls he usually never misses, throw his racquet, and scream at himself out loud for not listening to his mother and going to law school.

93

15. The "Run the Pro" or "I'll Hit the Ball at You, so You Can Hit it By Me" Drill

Another important drill designed for the more advanced players at the country club. Good acting skills are required. Drill may be better known by it's previous title: "Even though it's virtually impossible to win a point or game from me, I'm going to let you win one now and then so you'll come back next Wednesday morning and pay me another $65 an hour!"

16. The "You Actually Didn't Miss That Shot" Drill

The idea behind the drill is to give the country club student positive reinforcement. When playing points with him or her, the pro plays or volleys every shot the student hits – the ones that would be ten feet out, the ones that could be twenty feet wide, etc. – in the hopes that the student can ultimately win a point and feel good about him- or herself and, most importantly, the lesson he or she is taking. In the drill itself, when your student misses a particular shot (say a forehand), the pro quickly feeds or volleys another ball to the student's forehand and prays that he or she will eventually succeed at hitting his or her forehand in the court and hopefully forget how many forehands it took to actually get one in play.

17. The "Hit the Mercedes, Hit the Porsche" Drill

One of the most popular drills among the junior players at any country club, it's designed specifically for outdoor play. The country club pro should employ this exercise when his young students begin to lose interest in the lesson or clinic they're taking, which is usually about five or ten minutes after the pro has begun teaching! The idea of the drill is to get your junior players to work on the accuracy of their groundstrokes by having them smack tennis balls over the back fence and off the roof or trunk of one of the many Mercedes or Porsches in the parking lot. The country club pro can make a game of it by awarding points for each direct hit, bonus points if his or her students can set off a car alarm, or use creativity in any way they'd like. (At my club, any junior who could strike a passing golf cart and disrupt a member making a call on their cell phone would win the game automatically!)

18. The "Make the Country Club Member Suffer" Drill, Adult Female Jewish country club version: The "Make the JAP Sweat" Drill

An extremely important drill for the psychological wellbeing of the country club tennis professional. After countless hours of listening to your wealthy clientele talk about their latest trip to Europe, the lavish parties they've gone to every night that week, or the great handling on their new luxury SUV, the country club pro will need something to bring him out of his suicidal mood. The employment of the following drill can go a long way to stop the pro from throwing himself in front of the nearest train.

In the drill itself, instead of playing points where the ball is hit right at the student, as is usually done, the country club pro plays his student a little more realistically, running her corner to corner and baseline to net, hitting the ball just hard enough to keep the point going and the student moving. You'll know that you're playing these points properly when your student begins to convulse, gasp for air, and turn different shades of purple. During these intensely aerobic points, as you're running your student towards the point of collapse, I've found it extremely helpful to scream out things like, "Did you have a good time in Bermuda, bubby?"

Dear Mr. Country Club Tennis Pro,

I just played a set with one of your students here at the country club and a really strange thing kept happening. Every time I would miss a shot she would always have this forlorn expression on her face and say, "Two inches long." I'd miss a shot by three feet or six feet or an eighth of an inch and she'd always say, "Sorry, it was two inches long." After a while this was starting to drive me insane. Was this woman blind or what?

Signed,
Perplexed

Dear Perplexed,

Don't be alarmed. You're not losing your mind. It's important to remember, however, that at a Jewish country club, "two inches long" is the most commonly known unit of measurement. (You figure it out!)

Special Instructions When Working with Junior Players

The most embarrassing moment I ever had as a teaching pro occurred while I was teaching one of my junior clinics. I got distracted momentarily while I was feeding balls to one of my young students, an individual who, incidentally, had failed to make any contact at all on the previous thirty-six swings. Unfortunately for me, and for my desire to have any more children, she did manage to make contact on the thirty-seventh attempt, winding up and smashing what may have been the hardest forehand of her young life. (See photograph #12, pg. 131.)

Now, it should be pointed out that when any man is struck by an object traveling at a very high rate of speed in that very special place, the first inclination is to scream or cry, if one hasn't blacked out. Of course, when one is being closely watched by ten or twelve anxious parents and/or a host of admiring junior players, your tendency is to try and make it seem like nothing has actually happened. Like it's no big deal. Like you weren't really hit at all. As I was to discover, however, this can be a most formidable task, even for someone like myself who possesses superior acting skills.

97

"Are you okay? Are you okay, Mr. Tennis Man? How come you've got that funny look on your face?" little Sally Jacobs anxiously wanted to know.

"Sure, I'm all right, kid, heck of a shot," I groaned in a voice that might have landed me the role of Don Corleone in *The Godfather.*

"How come you're crying then? Did I do something wrong?" my student persisted, being acutely aware that her "Tennis Man" was normally a very happy and jovial fellow.

"Don't worry, honey, you hit a great shot! I'm so happy. I'm so happy you hit such a great shot that I'm crying. Doesn't your mommy sometimes cry because she's so happy?" I reasoned, trying to figure out how I was going to make my way off the court under my own power so I could find a hole to crawl in and die.

"Why is your face so red?" one of Sally's friends in the clinic wanted to know. "Do you have a tummy ache?"

"No, I feel great. Let's hit a few more forehands, okay?"

I moaned, glancing up nervously to see if any of the parents had observed my plight, wondering if I had ever experienced pain this excruciating before in my life.

"How come you're hunched over like that?" another of my young, observant juniors asked, laughing out loud.

A gathering crowd of students started to realize that something wasn't quite right with their tennis teacher.

"You look like this old horse we use to ride down at the farm! Hey, everybody, let's pile on the old horse!"

"Please don't, kids," I squealed in a voice with a much higher octave than when the clinic started, trying to limp to the door to avoid further embarrassment. But it was too late. And, as I lay smothered on a tennis court under the weight of eight or nine happy, laughing children, I wondered if it could ever get any worse than this. Yet, ever the optimist, I tried to look on the bright side.

"Hey," I thought to myself, "if I could never teach tennis again, or have another kid, I'm sure there'd be a place for me in the Mormon Tabernacle Choir!"

On my very first day at the country club – my very first junior clinic – after arriving two minutes late for the lesson, one of my seven-year-old students exclaimed, "Hey! Where were you? You're late! We're paying for this, you know!"

Now, one of my strengths as a teaching pro had always been the ability to be patient and not overreact in any given situation, but after a comment like that, from this spoiled little brat, I guess I kind of lost it.

99

"Oh, I'm two minutes late. Well, kid, let me first say, in the words of the great Steve Martin, 'Exxxcccuuussse meeeee!' And let's get one thing straight, little Jimmy, you're not paying for this lesson, Mommy is. And you know what? You and I are going to make up for me being late right now. Get your butt out on the court – let's go! Fifty balls side to side – move, move! Come on you little, @#$%&. You getting your money's worth now? Huh – what you outta breath, turning blue? Keep running!"

(I've got to work on that temper of mine.)

Every pro must have in his arsenal, if he is to succeed, tricks to impress the parents watching you give a lesson to their child. As in most cases, when the junior player has little or no ability, the country club pro needs to give the impression to the parents, especially after ninety-seven hours and $10,000 of your brilliant instruction, that there has been some improvement in their child. In the drill, bring your student up to net (groundstrokes are much to difficult) and feed nice easy high forehand volleys (no low volleys, too difficult – and no backhands!) and overheads (not to deep or high!). At my club I found it extremely useful to tell the student what was coming: "High volley now! Here comes another one – same place! Now an overhead – good! Wow, you're playing great today!" (Important Note: make certain the parent is not on the teaching court, or a lip reader.)

I did have an experience once where I thought I might not only lose my job, but also end up behind bars. I was teaching one of my top young female students and really running her around. I soon found out the hard way, however, that I was probably running her around too much.

"You're hurting my diaphragm! You're hurting my diaphragm!" she began yelling repeatedly, as the women on the adjoining court stopped playing and looked over at me in horror.

"What are you talking about?" I asked incredulously, trying to stay calm, realizing my teaching career might soon be in jeopardy if I didn't quickly handle the situation.

"You're hurting my diaphragm!" she wailed again through sobbing tears. A crowd of members started to gather around the court to hear her plea.

"Look, we're just hitting a few tennis balls, kid. I haven't gotten near you," I shot back defensively, nervously looking around to see if anyone believed my story.

"I'm going to tell my mommy that you hurt my diaphragm," she screamed back, dropping her racquet and covering her face with her hands.

"Look, sweetheart," I tried to reassure her, my mouth suddenly very dry, "we've just been working on some forehand and backhand groundstrokes. What have I done?"

101

"You're running me around too much and hurting my diaphragm, you know, in my throat. I learned that word in health class today. What did you think I was talking about?"

The look of relief must have been evident on my face as I wiped the sweat off my brow. Now, if only I had been wearing my Depends!

Dear Mr. Country Club Tennis Pro,

What did you mean yesterday when you said I had a "Yom Kippur forehand"?

Signed,
Lucille Mendelson

Dear Lucille,

What I was trying to say to you yesterday was that the only way you're ever going to get your forehand in the court was through a "@%#$LOAD OF PRAYER!"

102

Dear Mr. Country Club Tennis Pro,

I was playing next to you yesterday during one of your lessons and couldn't believe how rude the woman you were teaching was to you! Does that happen to you often at the country club?

Signed,
Marge Wollensky

Dear Marge,

Unfortunately, I do receive occasional comments from some of my students that might be considered a little rude. I thought you might be interested in a few of them.

1) "Hey, I got a great title for the book I hear you're writing that really says what you're all about: *Unforced Error: The Dan Waintrup Story!*"

2) (After saying to a student, "Remember we worked last week on turning your shoulders and hitting up on your serve?") "The only thing I want you to work on with me is seeing if you can shut your mouth for the entire lesson!"

3) (After making a disparaging remark about my forehand during a playing lesson with one of the club's better players.) "Hey, it's not fun if you put yourself down, that's what I like to do!"

4) (After remarking to one of my students, "You know, if we were in Palm Beach right now, this lesson wouldn't cost you $65, it would cost you $175.") "The only way I'd ever pay you $175 an hour is if you'd let me tie you up with duct tape, put an apple in your mouth, and see if I could smash it to pieces with my racquet!"

5) "You know that shrink you're seeing? I think it's time to ask for a refund!"

cont.

103

6)   (After remarking to my student, "You know, many people at the club say that playing with me is like playing with a ball machine because I'm so steady.") "I'd prefer a ball machine to you because ball machines can't talk!"

7)   (After hitting a great volley during a playing lesson with one of the club's better players and remarking, "A lot of people here at the club think I volley like Johnny Mac (John McEnroe).") "The only 'Mac' I think about when I see you volley is the one with 'Big' in front of it!"

8)   (After remarking to a student that one of the members had mentioned that I looked and played a lot like former Australian great Rod Laver.) "I think you misunderstood; he meant liver. You remind him of liver."

9)   (During a playing lesson, as one of my students was continually missing his passing shots every time I came up to net.)

CC Pro: You know, it's not unusual for my students to get nervous when I come to net.

Student: I wouldn't call it nervous; more like extreme nausea.

10) (After watching one of my assistant pros teaching one of my students because I wasn't available.)

cont.

CC pro to assistant pro: I guess it's pretty obvious who Mrs. Lebowitz's teaching pro has been the past few years.

Assistant pro: Unfortunately!

11) (After hitting a great slice backhand during a playing lesson with a country club member.)

CC pro: A lot of members in the club say I have the best slice they've ever seen.

CC member: There's only one "slice" I think about when I see you play, and it's got pepperoni on it!

12) (After hitting a winning forehand during a playing lesson with a member.)

CC pro: You know, I've heard people comment that I've got a forehand like Boris Becker's.

CC member: I think you misunderstood. They said you hit your forehand like a pecker, a pecker! Get yer ears checked, buddy!

13) (After missing an easy volley during a playing lesson.)

CC pro: (berating himself) Damn it! I've got the brain of a donkey!

CC member: Don't flatter yourself!

Dear Mr. Country Club Tennis Pro,

I know you may be the only rabbi's son in the world who plays tennis for a living, but I was just curious, do you think somewhere there is a minister's son just like you?

Signed,
Ted Tabinsky

Dear Ted,

It's interesting you should ask that question. I do have a friend in California who's a tennis pro and minister's son. We used to play together all the time back in college. Unfortunately, I think he's still a little upset from the last time we played when, after missing an easy forehand, I screamed, "Jesus Christ!"

Dear Mr. Country Club Tennis Pro,

I'm thirty-five years old now, but I still really enjoy playing those great young collegiate players. I guess my question to you is how do you know when it's finally time to start playing competitively with individuals in your own age group?

Signed,
Dan Abramawitz

Dear Dan,

You know it's time to start playing men your own age when you hear yourself saying "nice shot" to your opponent more than fifty-three times during the first set!

Dear Mr. Country Club Tennis Pro,

I was watching you talking to Mrs. Blumberg yesterday about the lesson you had just given to her daughter and was struck by how tactful and diplomatic you had to be. Would you say this is one of the most important attributes of a country club teaching pro?

Signed,
Carol Cohen

Dear Carol,

Certainly! Knowing how to talk to the membership at your club is important, although, in this particular situation, I don't think Mrs. Blumberg appreciated me telling her that the lesson I just had with her daughter reminded me of the movie From Here to Eternity.

Dear Mr. Country Club Tennis Pro,

I was playing on the court next to you during one of your lessons yesterday and was amazed at how much you talk during an hour of instruction. I was just wondering, with all the conversation over the years, have there ever been some things that you said on court that you wished you hadn't?

Signed,
Rachel Rabinowitz

Dear Rachel,

I've certainly made my share of stupid comments in the past. One time, near the end of a very long day of teaching, one of my students asked how long we'd been playing during her lesson and I remarked, "Oh, about $25 – I mean – 25 minutes!" Another time I was teaching a lesson right after I had come from my cousin's newborn son's circumcision ceremony at the Temple. After hitting a few balls with my student, I remarked, "How's your foreskin today, Mr. Goldberg?"

Dear Mr. Country Club Tennis Pro,

I was really shocked and surprised to come into the club last Sunday and see you teaching. I thought you had told me that it was your day off! It made me angry and upset because, if you remember, I asked you for a lesson on the very same day and you said that you couldn't do it. Can you clarify this situation for me?

Signed,
Pissed Off Peter

Dear Pissed Off Peter,

Normally I don't work on Sunday. However, the man I was teaching recently made the Fortune 500 list, and, as I told Mrs. Feingold, who had a similar question concerning my teaching availability, "If you were worth over $3 billion a year, I'd come in on my day off for you too, bubby!"

Dear Mr. Country Club Tennis Pro,

Did you ever get to read that book that came out years ago, *Racquet Back, Bend Your Knees, That Will Be $25 Please?*

Signed,
Ben Borman

Dear Ben,

Actually, I never did get a chance to read that book because I've been too busy working on my own version, *Racquet Back, (If You'd Like), Bend your Knees (If It Wouldn't Be an Inconvenience), That Will be $65 Please!* Of course, I guess it's all relative. When I was down in Palm Beach recently, at the Breakers Hotel, the book the pro there might write would be entitled, *Racquet Back, Bend your Knees, That Will Be $175 Please!* I mean I've heard of inflation, but that seems a little ridiculous to me. I've always complained to my friends about teaching tennis when it's 95 degrees, or really humid, or at 6 a.m., but for $175 an hour, I'd do back flips over the net and perform Beethoven's Fifth while standing on my head!

Dear Mr. Country Club Tennis Pro,

I had no idea what you were talking about in our lesson today! I know we were working on overheads and moving back from the net to leap up and smash those really tough lobs, but, for the life of me, I couldn't understand what you were trying to say to me. You kept talking about that Spike Lee movie, and did I see it, and didn't I think the acting was great... What does a Spike Lee movie have to do with me hitting overheads? I think you finally may have lost your mind!

Signed,
Peter Weisberg

Dear Peter,

Pete, what I was trying to tell you was that I think you could have had a starring role in that movie a few years back. You remember – White Men Can't Jump?

Dear Mr. Country Club Tennis Pro,

There have been rumors circulating around the club that you've been interviewing for other tennis positions. I can't believe that's true! I thought you loved it here at the country club! What do you have to say for yourself?

Signed,
The Tennis Chairman

Dear Mr. Chairman,

I must confess that I did interview last month at another club, during Chanukah, I believe. But don't worry – I don't believe it was really the right place for me. The people who were evaluating my teaching ability put me on a court with a women's clinic to see what kind of teaching pro I was, and I went into my familiar shtick.

"Okay, Mrs. Smith, let's get it going! Let's move to the ball! You've got to react to the shot, sweetheart. I've seen Menorahs move faster!" The deafening silence that followed the comment was indescribable. You could have heard a pin drop. And then, the words that I'll always remember, "What's a Menorah?"

Celebrity Correspondence

Dear Mr. Country Club Tennis Pro,

I saw you teaching Aaron Wein-
stein yesterday and, boy, did he look
terrible. He must have had a hell of
a lot to drink the night before! How
do you teach your students when
they're so hungover?

Signed,
Ted Kennedy

Dear Ted,

VERY QUIETLY!

113

Dear Mr. Country Club Tennis Pro,

I really think the use of videotape
is the best way to improve. I've
had some experience with it in
the past, but wanted to get a
professional's opinion.

Signed,
Paris Hilton

Dear Paris,

I've seen some of
your work. Call me!

Dear Mr. Country Club Tennis Pro,

I was watching the US Open this year and was extremely upset when I heard the announcer saying, "Mr. Agassi has loved thirty," and "Mr. Agassi has loved forty." I mean it's no one's business how many women Mr. Agassi has had a personal relationship with! Citizens in this great country of ours are afforded certain rights and privileges guaranteed by the Constitution of the United States of America!

Signed,
President George W. Bush
(Your Commander and Chief)

Dear Mr. President,

I know I have the sentiment of every individual in the entire country when I say, "Please, God, don't let anything bad happen to Dick Cheney!"

Dear Mr. Country Club Tennis Pro,

I love working with children! I've noticed you have many junior clinics, and I would love helping you out some time if you ever needed it, because I love children and love being around them and... You know how it is...

Signed,
Michael Jackson

Dear Michael,

I know you were acquitted, but...

Dear Mr. Country Club Tennis Pro,

I know that your women's doubles teams have had another great year, and part of their success must be attributed to your ability to motivate them to play their best during their interclub matches. In your many years of experience as a women's team coach, what have you found to be the most helpful or constructive pre-match advice for your team?

Signed,
Billy Jean King

Dear Billy Jean,

I've found the best coaching advice to be the simplest coaching advice: "DON'T @#$%&ING MISS!"

Special Instructions When Working with My Beautiful Girls

Dear Mr. Country Club Tennis Pro,

I heard you were trying to write a book about your experiences as a country club tennis pro. Could you give me an idea of what it would be about?

Signed,
Sally Gould

Dear Sally,

At this time, I really wouldn't want to reveal the content of the book, although I'm certain you'll be able to relate to some to the chapters I'm working on: "Jewish Women Don't Run Backwards," "Winning Without Guilt," "Country Club Tennis Workout: Sweating Out the Foie Gras."

Dear Mr. Country Club Tennis Pro,

I know you've had some great women's doubles teams here at the club the past few years. What have been some of the keys to their success?

Signed,
Evelyn Moskowitz

Dear Evelyn,

We have had some excellent teams here recently. It took some time to realize, however, that if they were to be successful, I would have to learn to motivate them a little differently than if I were working with a team from a regular tennis club. For example, it took me some time before I understood how to get my girls to manage the pressures and highly stressful situations that often occur in a match, by making certain they remembered that, even if they were to lose, they were still the better-dressed team! In time, I was able to get my teams to avoid breakdowns in concentration and win their matches more quickly by telling them that if they didn't plan on being victorious in straight sets, then they might miss the sale! And, after many years of trial and error, I discovered how to get my ladies to play smarter and more efficiently on clay court surfaces, by reminding them if they came up to net, angled their volleys, and ended the points sooner, then they'd have a better chance of not getting their pretty little outfits dirty!

When teaching a women's clinic at a country club, it's important for the pro not to get overly concerned or upset by his or her students' general lack of desire in running for the ball, or, as we pros would say, in "bouncing on their toes." As one exasperated woman explained the inability to perform this task so clearly, "How do you expect me to run? I just had a pedicure!" In time, you'll learn to hit the ball right at your students, about waist high, so they don't have to move.

The country club tennis pro must also remember to forget trying to teach the standard "ready position" to the new female clientele. In time, the pro will realize that there is no ready position for the majority of his or her students, just a bored, far away look many of these women will show you as they are deep in thought about one of society's most pressing problems – what color to paint the cabinets in their newly-remodeled kitchen!

Most people don't realize that there is a distinct difference between the traditional ready position and the country club ready position.

And last, but certainly not least, it's extremely important for the country club tennis pro to remember that the women that he or she will now be working with will rarely have the time or desire to pick up the tennis balls during or after a lesson or clinic. Looking for an explanation for this strange phenomenon on my first day of teaching at the club, one of the women I was teaching exclaimed, "Please, I just had my nails done!" If the unthinkable happens during an instructional period, and one of your students ruins her manicure, be prepared to offer counseling and a full refund.

To help the country club pro in the teaching of women's clinics, I've written out a curriculum of one of my most recent ones:

119

10:30 a.m.   Clinic officially starts. (Pro must allow ten minutes for clinic participants to talk about their latest trips south or abroad.)

10:45 a.m.   Get the women on court (the ones that show up!). Pro should allow five minutes for students to take off jewelry and Ellesse warm-ups.

10:50 a.m.   Ten minutes of easy forehands and backhands. (No running!)

11:00 a.m.   Water break! (Women will be exhausted from all the aerobic activity.)

11:05 a.m.   Clinic resumes. (Pro should allow five minutes for women to discuss important world issues and events – the cost of Mrs. Goldstein's son's Bar Mitzvah.)

11:10 a.m.   Women work on rallying, while trying not to run, sweat, or break their nails.

11:20 a.m.   Water break! (Women will be exhausted from all the aerobic activity.)

11:30 a.m.   Students play doubles. (Pro concentrates on attempting not to offend anyone.)

11:45 a.m.   Clinic officially ends for half the women who have to leave early for an "urgent appointment." (Translation: lunch or shopping.)

11:50 a.m.   Pro picks up all tennis balls as women talk about the caterer Mrs. Goldstein is going to sue for overcharging her for her son's Bar Mitzvah.

Noon   Clinic officially ends. (Pro should not be alarmed by the nervous twitch or receding hairline that seems to have developed since he started doing these women's clinics.)

Dear Mr. Country Club Tennis Pro,

You pros have the life. I know that you've taught hundreds of beautiful, gorgeous women in your country club teaching career and am certain that you have probably been propositioned a million times! I must know — is it true? Have you had many women try to pick you up over the years?

Signed,
Jealous George

Dear George,

I hate to burst your bubble, bubby, but this whole idea that tennis pros have scores of women dying to have affairs with them is just a huge fallacy. I must admit, however, that over the years, there have been a number of comments made to this county club teaching professional that could be misinterpreted as somewhat suggestive in nature:

1) "I love playing with your Thunderstick!"
(To the casual observer, the above statement could be viewed in a sexual context, although most knowledgeable tennis players are aware that the individual commenting was just remarking how much she liked playing with one of the tennis pro's demo racquets from years ago, Prince's Racquet Company's, "Thunderstick.")

2) "I need to have my legs sucked."
(What appears to be an overtly sexual demand from one of my female students, is actually just a frequent

cont.

121

lament by some of the women I've taught at the country club through the years of their need to tone up those legs the quickest way they know how, with some liposuction!)

3) "I need to be drilled by you."
(In this case, one of my students is actually requesting to be worked very hard by the tennis professional on a specific part of her game, although the statement could be viewed in a more suggestive fashion.)

4) "Can I play with your balls?"
(Again, to the untrained ear, the preceding statement could be viewed as some kind of sexual request, although most intelligent tennis players are aware that the "balls" the individual is asking for are marked "Wilson" or "Pro Penn.")

Dear Mr. Country Club Tennis Pro,

We are so embarrassed! My partner and I thought we were going to blow these women off the court in our doubles match. I guess we just underestimated them. Is there any advice you can give us so we don't make the same mistake in the future? Is there any way to know if you're in for a really tough match, even if you've never seen your opponents play before?

Signed,
Debby and Doreen
(Your No. 1 Team!)

Dear Debby and Doreen,

You can probably assume you're in for a tough match when your opponents have deeper voices and more facial hair than the majority of the members of the USC men's varsity tennis team! (See photograph #14, pg. 132.)

Debby and Doreen – The Female Student's Perspective

The country club tennis pro's favorite doubles team – Debby and Doreen – have a conversation over lunch:

Debby: I am beginning to question whether I should continue my lessons here at the club. What do you think of the pro?

Doreen: Well, he's a lot nicer than the last guy. I told the General Manager the other day what a great decision it was to bring Dan on board.

Debby: You know the GM doesn't seem to be here very much lately.

Doreen: Oh he's here... Just in the background. I think you just don't notice him as much when Dan's around.

Doreen: Well, I'll tell you this much, I certainly must have made our pro happy with all the lessons I've taken from him the last couple of years.

Debby: And all the clothes I've bought in his pro shop...

Doreen: And all my friends who have taken lessons from him...

Debby: And that Porsche! He used to drive a Datsun – He owes us big time!

Doreen: He's such a flirt though, always saying suggestive things...

Debby: Yeah, like last week at practice, my Vibrazorb fell out of my racquet and he asked, "Do you want me to put your 'vibrator' back in for you?"

Doreen: He didn't!

Debby: I swear! Ask Sheryl Blumberg. She was right there.

Doreen: That's nothing! I told him I wanted to do some filming – you know, videotape my forehand – so he goes, "I'd love to videotape you. Maybe later at the Marriott?"

Debby: He must have been joking!

Doreen: I don't think so...

Debby: He's just a guy; you know they only think about one thing. And he probably thinks he's giving us a thrill.

Doreen: He's a rabbi's son, right? Unbelievable!

Debby: Did you hear Dan recently became single again?

Doreen: So rumor has it. I swear the only reason Mrs. Lebowitz keeps taking lessons from him is that she's hoping he will get interested in Sylvia...

Debby: Poor Sylvia, is she back from her "spa" vacation?

Doreen: Next week. You know, I think Dan is really sucking up to Morty Levine trying to get a job in his Wall Street office. Morty has won three matches against Dan in the last two weeks. Prior to that, I don't think he had won more than a few points against him.

Debby: You know Morty and I were joking about that at the ballet gala last week. Morty said his Board of Directors would call a no confidence vote if he brought Dan into the company. He said, "Waintrup thinks venture capital is the newest theme park outside of DC and an IPO is something you make with Smirnoff."

Doreen: I guess we won't see Dan out of his tennis whites for a while.

Debby: Those white shirts make his eyes look so blue...

Doreen: Were Libby and Seth at the ballet gala?

Debby: Yes, and Libby looked awful. She has got to get a grip. She is compulsively buying tennis racquets in the pro shop! I think she has bought ten in the last few months. She just cannot get past her fertility issues. And you know the funny part is Dan thinks it's because he is the world's greatest salesman.

Doreen: Well, you know who I'm feeling badly for is poor old Mo. He's really starting to lose it. Sometimes I get the feeling that he really thinks he can hit the ball.

Debby: Dan is really good with him though. He must be a great dad.

Doreen: Did you see Dan's son when he was here the other afternoon? They look so much alike. He was giving his son a lesson – do you think he charges him?

Debby: Dan is pretty amazing as a player. And he has been very complimentary of my progress on the court. He says I am his most inspiring student.

Doreen: Hey, he said the same thing to me. Do you think we're being conned?

Debby: I wouldn't care if we could just win a few doubles matches.

Doreen: I don't know what it is! We always play great with him in practice…

Debby: Yeah, we never miss those high forehand volleys and short overheads he feeds us.

Doreen: But when we play our matches, the ball never goes there. It comes to our backhands, or they hit it low, or even a couple of feet away from us…

Debby: Or sometimes right at us! How are we supposed to get those shots?

Doreen: I said to the girls we played last week, "Hey – what are you doing? We haven't worked on that shot yet. Hit it here like our pro does, to the forehand side."

Debby: They didn't want to do that. They were really mean. They looked at us like we were crazy!

Doreen: I asked Dan what should we do. He said, "Don't worry. We'll work on those shots next week."

Debby: He's been saying that for two years. I am really beginning to wonder if this is some kind of racket…

Doreen: I've been taking lessons with him for five years, and I still can't hit the ball in the court more than two times in a row.

Debby: Yeah, but he's cute.

Doreen: And those eyes…

Debby: And he says I'm really starting to make some progress…

Many country club professionals have found that knee pads can have other uses

128

Dear Mr. Country Club Tennis Pro,

What do you think of my game?

Signed,
Joan Rosen

Dear Joan,

Well, you know, Joan, your tennis game kind of reminds me of that MasterCard commercial. 100 lessons taken last year: $6,500

10 top-of-the-line racquets purchased in my pro shop: $2,500

5 of the most expensive tennis outfits on the market sold to you: $850

You not showing up for our weekly lesson: PRICELESS!

Dear Mr. Country Club Tennis Pro,

If my game were a song, what would it be?

Signed,
Debby Dorfman

Dear Debby,

Oh, Debby, that's an easy one. Remember that AC/DC song from the '70s – "Highway to Hell"?

Dear Mr. Country Club Tennis Pro,

How do you know when you're getting a little too old to play competitive tennis?

Signed,
Rachel Gould

Dear Rachel,

You know it's probably time to hang up the old tennis sneakers when:

1) You no longer play to win, but to have a "good sweat,"

2) You consider the match you're playing a success if you get through it without injury,

3) Your main goal when playing a set with someone is not to embarrass yourself.

Dear Mr. Country Club Tennis Pro,

If you had to make a list of the five things that you hate to hear most as a tennis teacher here at the country club, what would they be?

Signed,
Rebecca

130

Dear Rebecca,

Certainly there are many things that have caused me to go prematurely bald here at the club, but if I had to list the top five, they'd be the following:

1) "Wow, I can't believe how much more I learned from your assistant when I took a lesson from him."

2) "You know, it's strange, but I haven't had a lesson with you in months, and I've never played better."

3) "Darn, I forgot my wallet again, do you mind if I pay you for the lesson next week?"

4) "Sorry, was that your brand new racquet I just cracked?"

5) "Your 2:30 lesson just cancelled because his arm is still killing him from the lessons you gave him last week."

6) "You're fired."

#12.

"While I appear happy in this photo, moments later one of my young juniors would strike me with a forehand in that 'special area,' forcing me to consider a career as a soprano."

#13.

"Here I am giving some encouragement to one of my young students before he participates in the well known country club drill – Crawl to the Ball."

14

AP/Wide World Photos

132

"Some of the opponents my country club girls have
to play in their doubles matches may have a
steroid problem."

5. Old Pros Never Die, They Just Go to Business School

Dear Mr. Country Club Tennis Pro,

You almost killed me today! What are you, crazy? I almost had a &*%@#ing heart attack! Do you work all your students this hard?

Signed,
Robert Sternberg

Dear Robert,

Only the ones that continually forget their MasterCard, bubby!

It Starts with the Knees

There came a time in my country club teaching career when I truly felt that I couldn't continue to do it full-time any longer. Teaching tennis and being on court eight to ten hours a day, six or seven days a week, forty-eight to fifty weeks a year, was really starting to take its toll on me, not just mentally, but physically as well.

The stark reality was that I wasn't twenty-five years old anymore. I wasn't that young, energetic kid fresh out of college who could teach all day and party all night. The intensely physical and debilitating nature of the job was causing my mind and body to break down. (See photograph #16, pg. 164.)

134

The biggest problem I encountered when I was teaching a long stretch of hours was the deterioration in my ability to effectively instruct my students. Normally, I'm an extremely encouraging and unusually patient tenni-teaching professional. However, I clearly remember an incident that I am not proud of. Earlier on that particular day, during Cindy Karp's lesson, I showed the patience of a saint as she missed volley after volley at the net.

"Don't worry about the errors," I said with a soothing smile, "just keep that racquet head up and moving forward with your wrist locked in a short punching motion and I know you'll get it!"

But by the end of the day, Cindy's friend Betsy displayed the same ineptitude at the net and my usually tolerant attitude had vanished.

"Let's face it, sweetheart, you just can't do it," I shouted sarcastically, "Maybe mahjong or bridge might be a little more up your alley!"

I don't mean to imply that the long, grueling hours on a tennis court were beginning to make me meaner and a little impatient, but there was a rumor going around the club that day about a new teaching pro and his name was Saddam! Mo Weinberg, my final student of the day, might have agreed with that assessment. "Okay, buddy, I know you just turned ninety, and you just had the triple bypass, but were gonna run 'til it hurts, now move it!"

I started to get sick more than I usually would, often losing my voice for days at a time. I'd joke to my students that if I were a horse, they'd shoot me. What good is a tennis pro without his voice!? (Of course, it certainly didn't help my morale much when some of my students told me that the best lesson they ever had with me was when I couldn't say a word to them!)

As I approached forty, my knees started to fail me. I started wearing kneepads for support. There were days when my back hurt so bad that I had trouble getting out of bed unless I had some help from my two best friends, Motrin and Advil. The situation was exacerbated by the fact that the majority of my clientele were good players and preferred playing games and sets with an opponent who could give them a real challenge on the court – me. Whether they booked me at seven in the morning or seven at night, their goal was to run around, sweat, get a good workout and have a few laughs; they weren't going to pay me to stand at the net and feed them tennis balls.

135

Unfortunately, with each passing year, this was getting tougher and tougher to do. It was becoming increasingly more difficult to give my clientele the challenge they expected on the court.

The wear and tear of being on a tennis court for so many hours during my country club tennis career has certainly had it's effect on me physically

I knew I had to find a solution to the problem. I certainly didn't want to have a heart attack during a lesson with Morty Levine or Mrs. Lebowitz. What else could I do to make money? I had heard that some of my fellow pros, aging comrades in the same boat, had cut down on their hours on court and were selling houses on the weekend. A part-time career in residential real estate? Maybe that was something I could do. After all, I reasoned, as a tennis pro, I was always selling something, whether it was myself as a teacher, or merchandise from my pro shop. Selling homes, selling racquets, it seemed logical enough. I got my real estate license and joined a local firm, eager to make some extra cash.

I was desperate for my first sale and booked an appointment with a client who could only go out and see listings on Sunday nights. She had seen this "fantastic" house advertised in the paper and was "absolutely certain" that this was the one she wanted to buy. This client had dragged me to twenty "fantastic" houses during the last year that she had seen advertised in the paper and that she was "absolutely certain" she wanted to buy. But they all proved to be false alarms.

Even though it was ten degrees below zero, I reluctantly agreed to show her the house, hoping that maybe this was the one, but I was sure it would probably be a waste of time like all the others. (Important: most residential real estate salespeople do a lot of hoping. The majority of them work on commission!) We somehow managed to find the house through the cold and snow on an old, deserted country road. The house was vacant and the electricity shut off. "This is going to be so much fun," I thought to myself, as I took out my old trusty flashlight and we headed through the front door.

"This is the living room," I muttered as I tried to read the listing sheet in the dark, "I think."

"I can't really see anything. Maybe we should come back tomorrow when it's light out. This place is really scary," my client whispered through the dark, frigid air.

137

"Yeah, let's come back tomorrow," I agreed, wondering how I was going to blow off an afternoon of lessons to show this women a house she probably wasn't going to put an offer on anyway.

Just then, as we started to make our way out of the house, we heard the sound of a dog barking. It sounded big, mean, and like it was coming toward us. My client and I were both scared out of our minds.

"It sounds like it could be a German Shepherd or a pit bull. Let's get out of here!" I shrieked, both of us sprinting for our respective cars.

Unfortunately, in my haste, I failed to notice a flight of stairs, which I proceeded to fall down face first. A sharp pain shot through my back, but the sound of the dog seemed to be getting closer and closer. I somehow managed to get to my feet and limp to my car. Turning on the car light I noticed I had ripped my pants and shirt. I was bleeding in various places, and my back was killing me. "But at least I avoided being attacked by that huge dog," I thought to myself, trying to look on the bright side.

The next day my back was even worse. I would subsequently find out that I had cracked two ribs in my fall – an injury that would make running and hitting tennis balls an extremely painful experience over the next few months. Of course, this pain was nothing compared to going back to the house I had attempted to show my client the following day and realizing that the massive creature that was going to attack us and eat us alive was actually a little Chihuahua tied up on a leash next door!

I did make another desperate attempt to get a listing – and this is a moment I am really not proud of. My best friend was married to a very beautiful woman, who unfortunately contracted breast cancer and passed away. In keeping with the Jewish tradition, my friend sat *shiva* in their lovely home while friends and family dropped by in an attempt to give comfort and support. I arrived to give my condolences. As I approached my friend I handed him my real estate card and said, "Has it occurred to you that this house might feel a little too big now? You might want to consider moving."

If anyone other than me had made the joke, he probably would have laid them out, but because it was me he just laughed and understood the spirit in which the joke was intended.

But that was the end of my real estate career! I clearly did not have what it takes to succeed.

And I still hadn't solved my dilemma. How was I going to teach less, preserve my mental and physical health, and still make enough money to support a wife and two young kids? After months of uncertainty and endless suggestions from friends and family ("No, Dad, I still don't think rabbinic seminary is the answer."), I decided that business school and an MBA weren't such bad ideas after all. A couple of my fellow teaching pros convinced me that getting an MBA would give me the chance to stay in tennis, but be on court less, by helping me develop skills that would be more applicable to the financial and management aspects of the business. Who knows, maybe someday, with all this knowledge, I could own my own tennis club.

It seemed like a good idea. My mother was certainly thrilled: "Thank God! He's finally going back to school… I can die happy!"

Going back to school at forty can have its drawbacks and being away from the discipline of a classroom for twenty years can have its awkward moments… Like not having any idea how to use a computer. I didn't think it was such a big deal. When the professor in my first business class assigned a paper, I figured I would merely whip out my old Smith Corona to get the job done. But when he handed back the papers, I found out the hard way that this was probably not a very wise decision.

"Class, I'd like you all to know that even though it may be the dawn of the new millennium, there are still people out there in this wonderful, dynamic technological age of ours, amazingly enough, who don't know how to use a computer," my professor began.

An ominous feeling gathered in the pit of my stomach.

"Is there a Mr. Waintrup in the room tonight?"

"Ahh, yes, that's me, sir," I stammered over the words, acutely aware that there were maybe forty to fifty pairs of incredulous and disbelieving eyes looking my way.

"Now, Mr. Waintrup, you do know how to use a computer, don't you?"

"Well, actually I haven't had the time to learn. I was going to have someone…"

"I'm just dying to know, have you been living in a cave the last ten years?"

"No sir, I just never had the chance to…"

"Mr. Waintrup, I'm not interested in your personal problems. I strongly suggest you learn how to use a computer or else I think you're going to have a very difficult time getting through this class and getting your degree. Do I make myself perfectly clear?"

"Hey, no problem, sir, I'll redo the paper and have it on your desk tomorrow morning," I mumbled, wondering how many different shades of red and purple I was turning.

"You can email it to me. You do know how to use email, don't you, Mr. Waintrup?"

"Oh sure, everyone knows how to use email, right," I lied, wondering who the hell I was going to find in the next twenty-four hours to teach me to use a computer and send an email.

I remember thinking after this wonderful exchange, "Isn't this nice? I feel like I'm back in third grade. I'd forgotten what it was like to be embarrassed and humiliated in front of a group of people."

It certainly was an interesting way to start my business school career. Ultimately, I learned to use a computer and email and graduated from business school. Many of my friends were greatly impressed with this accomplishment. "Flabbergasted" might be a better word. "Completely and totally stunned" was actually the term I heard most often.

"Let me get this straight," an old college friend said, calling me up upon hearing the news, "You were a history major in college. I mean, even that statement is a joke when you think about it. The only thing you really majored in at college was chasing blondes and drinking beer. Everyone knows that you haven't picked up a book in at least fifteen years."

"That's not true!" I protested, "I just recently finished *Touchdown for Tommy!*"

But he continued. "The only thing you've done since 1980 is hit tennis balls ten hours a day. You're truthfully going to sit there and tell me that you have an MBA?"

"That is correct," I stated proudly and triumphantly.

"Dan, come on," another friend started, "the last time I checked, you couldn't multiply five by six. How in the hell did you get a business degree?! You must have paid somebody right? How much did it cost? You can level with us. We're your friends. Nobody has to know what really happened."

In truth, I couldn't blame my friends for their skepticism. I had certainly never in my life given any indication to anyone that I had any financial or business skills of any kind. Outside my immediate family and relatives, there literally wasn't anyone who thought I had what it took to get an MBA.

"Maybe I'm a little smarter than you think," I offered to all those people who didn't think I could do it. Of course, I tried to explain to them I was helped greatly by the fact that half of every class grade in the courses I took in business school was group projects. And, over the course of the graduate program I was in, Dan Waintrup became extremely adept at identifying the most intelligent people in the class he was taking, and getting on their team. You know, it's that old adage, "If you're not sure how to get to the finish line, at least be smart enough to get on the horse that knows how to get there!"

143

In the real world, the key to the success of any group of people is to assemble a team of individuals who know their roles, understand their defined functions, and are willing to work together towards a common goal. There was never any doubt that I knew what my role was.

"Hey Fred, I think you may be a little better at the financial stuff. You do the spreadsheet, and I'll buy the sushi."

Trust me, every group that I was part of was the happiest and best fed on campus. I made certain that there was never going to be anyone on any of the teams that I participated in who was ever going to be hungry or thirsty.

"Gee, Lori, that section you're doing on the statistical derivatives and analytical assumptions inherent in the financial services industries of Germany, England, and France between 1985 and 1995 is really coming along. Could I get you another white chocolate mocha cappuccino grande latte?"

Interestingly enough, over time my role evolved from buying my fellow group members dinner and coffee to the guy who kept everyone loose. I became the individual who kept everyone focused on and working towards the successful completion of the task at hand.

And it didn't hurt that I was usually the best writer in the group.

144

Of course the question still remained. Now that I had this vast amount of business knowledge and a fancy degree, what was I going to do with it? How could I apply my MBA to make more money and, hopefully, improve the quality of my life?

In a perfect world, I had hoped to find an opportunity in the tennis world that could take advantage of my newly developed management and financial skills. Unfortunately, when I got out of business school, there weren't any positions in the area I lived that could utilize the new knowledge that I now possessed. A friend of the family suggested that I continue teaching tennis, but come work for him building a client base of high net worth individuals and families for his investment company.

"You'll be a natural," my new boss said. "With your selling and networking skills, and all the wealthy people you know, I think you'll do very well."

"Yeah, why not," I said reassuringly. At this point I was willing to try almost anything.

"I'll go with you on the first few sales calls, just so you can get an idea of the pitch. Just remember, you're a pretty funny guy, but nobody is going to give $5 million to Jackie Mason, got it?"

"Sure, no problem. Hey I can play it straight if I have to – let's give it a shot," I replied, excited about the possibility of a new career and the chance to make some real money.

Approaching the "estate" of our first potential client, I couldn't help but notice something strangely familiar about the house. I felt like I'd seen it before, but I couldn't quite place it in my mind.

"Doesn't this house look familiar, boss? Haven't we seen this somewhere before?"

"No, I don't think so. It doesn't matter. Alright, we're here, now stick to the script. Remember, no jokes."

He rang the doorbell. As it opened it suddenly occurred to me.

"I got it, the house on the *Addams Family*! Remember that show where those strange people lived in that old, haunted castle and…"

"Dan, please…"

"May I help you, gentleman?" the tall, ghostly looking butler interrupted.

"And you must be Lurch, the butler. It's uncanny!" I blurted out, wishing I had kept the thought to myself.

"I told you no comedy!" my boss whispered angrily. He was getting a little aggravated.

"Sorry, but he looks just like the guy!" I started to explain.

"I don't give a @#$%&* who he looks like. This family is worth over $50 million. Keep your mouth shut!"

We made our way into the house and it was like we were entering another world – like we were entering an old, medieval mansion. Works of Renaissance art and sculptures were positioned side-by-side with strange antiques and paintings from many different eras. Strange color combinations and weird architectural forms were everywhere. A couple of dogs and cats wandered aimlessly amidst the clutter. My thoughts about the bizarre interior of the house were interrupted by the voice of my boss.

"Mr. Smith – How are you? Thanks for taking the time to invite us into your wonderful home. This is my associate, Daniel Waintrup. He'll be joining us today for the meeting."

Looking around I couldn't contain myself.

"I love what you've done with the house, sir. What would you call it? Neo-psychotic European fourth-century art deco?" A look of shock crossed my boss's face.

"Excuse me, young man, what was that you said?" our potential client asked, thankfully adjusting his hearing aid and missing the majority of my comment.

"Oh, love what you've done with the house. Very interesting."

147

"Why, thank you. Shall we begin the meeting?"

My new boss leaned over to me as we sat down. "One more crack like that and you'll be selling houses again in the middle of February. You understand me?"

"Got it, no more Jackie Mason, sorry."

Fortunately for me that day, I stopped doing stand-up, we made the sale, and I made a very nice commission.

Maybe, just maybe, I had finally found something that could complement my tennis teaching career.

Dear Mr. Country Club Tennis Pro,

I hear you've been doing some work for an investment company. Have you ever played tennis with any of its clients?

Signed,
Mel Nussbaum

148

Dear Mel,

Actually, I just recently played a few sets with one of our top investors. Some of the individuals who have given money to the investment company that I've been working for are pretty good players, and, from time to time, I'll go out and hit a few balls with them. Logically, if one of your company's clients has given you a great deal of money to invest, your inclination is to give them the benefit of the doubt on those close line calls. Recently, I was playing a set with one of the company's top investors and he hit a ball that could have been called either in or out. When he asked whether his shot was good or not, I responded, "Mr. Levine, I can give you five million reasons why that shot was good!"

Dear Mr. Country Club Tennis Pro,

What was the most frustrating lesson you ever gave?

Signed,
Harriet Cohen

Dear Harriet,

That would have to be the time I was teaching ninety-year-old Mo Weinberg. Now, you should know that I love Mo to death (maybe a bad choice of words when talking about a ninety-year-old?), but God, I wish he had a better hearing aid.

"Okay, Mo, we're going to work on some forehands today."

"What?"

"Forehands, Mo, we're going to work on some fore-hands."

"I got something on my forehead? What's on my forehead?"

"No, Mo, listen! Forehands, your forehand, that's what I said, you're not listening..."

"What do you mean I'm a sorehead? I'm no sore-head. Let me tell you something, young man, I've

cont.

149

been playing this game before you were in diapers, and I don't appreciate your attitude towards..."

"No, Mr. Weinberg, I didn't call you a sorehead. I just want to work on your FOREHAND. YOUR FORE-HAND!"

"Alright, alright, you don't have to yell. I can hear you. That's all I've wanted to do the last ten min-utes, but first you say I have something on my forehead, and then you call me a sorehead! What's a student to think for christsakes?"

"Lord, give me strength."

"You want to give me a rake? I thought we were going to hit a few forehands?"

The best thing about my country club tennis program is the young, dynamic, nature of many of my students, as we see here in a picture from the last tournament I had, "The CPR Invitational"

Waintrup's Rules for Winning
What Kind of Forehand Do You Have?

There are three ways to hit a tennis ball: flat (no spin), topspin (overspin), and slice (underspin).

Which way is best for you? Well, bubby, that depends on numerous factors, most notably, your coordination level, your age, your goals in tennis, and what you do naturally.

When teaching a student for the first time, I'd usually begin the lesson by rallying with him or her for a few minutes and then say, "So what kind of forehand do you have?" It always amazed me how often I'd hear, "I'm not sure..."

"Well," I'd continue, "If you don't know what kind of forehand you're hitting, how are you controlling the ball?"

"I'm not certain, I've never really thought about it. I'm just hitting it."

"I see, so if your forehand goes long or in the net, you have no idea how to correct that, or what it really means."

"Yeah, that's right, I guess so..."

"Well, you know what, Mrs. Robbins, I think you and I are going to be spending a lot of time together the next few months!"

I must admit, over the years it was incredible to this county club tennis professional how often my first-time students were completely unaware of the ground-strokes they hit and how they actually controlled the ball on a tennis court. What I tried to get across to them was that, in essence, good tennis – consistent tennis - was all about learning how to control their shots on a tennis court. What I tried to get across to them was that the better you are as a tennis player, the better you are at ball control.

The reality is, for the majority of the players I've taught in my county club teaching career, the most natural way for someone to hit a tennis ball, and usually the most common way for first-time students and beginners, is to hit through the ball, flat, with no spin. Unfortunately for them, but not for this country club pro (I am now able to make the down payment on the new Porsche), hitting the ball flat is almost always the most inconsistent way to play the game.

Why? The answer to that question relates to the most fundamental aspect of the game of tennis, which is to hit the ball over a certain barrier (the net), and within a certain boundary (the baseline and/or sideline). Unless you were born with the superhuman hand-eye coordination, vision, and racquet control of someone like Jimmy Connors, the chances of any player being able to hit the ball flat, with no spin, more than three times in a row consistently, are pretty slim. Hitting a ball this way doesn't give you much "margin for error."

That's why, as I like to say, the good Lord on the eighth day invented topspin. That's why he invented this wonderful shot where you swing your racquet, where you swing your vertical racquet face low to high through contact, causing the ball to literally "spin over its top." The great thing about topspin is that it causes the ball to dip. It forces the ball to go down when hit correctly. Theoretically, topspin allows you to consistently arc your shots over the barrier and within that boundary. Someone who is proficient at topspin should be able to beat someone who can only hit the ball flat, with no spin. And certainly, few would argue against the idea that if you're going to be a truly advanced player in tennis, that if you're going to be a great offensive player, that you need to have topspin in your repertoire.

I have to admit that over the years, however, I've found underspin, the third way to hit a tennis ball, to be a far more prevalent and natural way for many to hit a groundstroke, and a far easier shot for students to learn. Slice is topspin's direct opposite, the natural counteraction to it, the most obvious difference being that when you hit with underspin, when you hit down on the ball, you're forcing the ball to spin under its axis. If a student came on my teaching court with a natural slice, unlike many pros, I would never take that away from him. I would show him the other ways to hit a ball, but I made certain that we worked on making his slice better. I made sure that we'd work on improving the shot he hit "naturally."

154

One of my favorite students, ninety-year-old Mo Weinberg, had a natural slice that he'd been hitting for fifty years. Mo didn't have the time, desire, or ability to learn topspin, so I never forced it on him. Instead, our time together was spent working to improve his underspin game; it was spent working to get him to be able to hit the shot more consistently in different situations, and off of balls coming at him at varying speeds, spins, and heights. (Of course, my most important goal when working with Mr. Weinberg was to get through the entire lesson without having to call 911!)

As a player, I always felt that slice was the most underrated and under-appreciated of the three groundstrokes. And in truth, I felt this way not just because it was the first way I learned to hit a ball, and not because it's the most "natural" way for me to hit a ball, but because I was able to drive the majority of the opponents I played in my life absolutely crazy with it. The reasons for this are obvious if you think about it. Underspin, when hit correctly, is the perfect counter stroke, the perfect counteraction to topspin. My opponents would hit their high, bouncing, powerful topspin drives and I would play inside the baseline, taking them "on the rise," intercepting their shots with my natural high to low groundstrokes, using their pace and energy to drive the ball back. If you are in shape and understand the mechanics of the slice and how to hit it off of various speeds and heights, it can be a very effective shot.

155

"You're nothing but a pusher!"

"You're a hacker!"

"Don't you know how to play the game?"

"You suck!"

I can't begin to tell you the insults and put downs I'd hear after the many matches I played, but the truth was, I won a lot more than I lost with this style over the years.

Topspin, flat, slice... The best way to hit a tennis ball? In a perfect world, you should be able to execute all three on a tennis court. You need to learn how to control hitting the ball in different ways if you want to achieve your true potential as a tennis player. The more ways you can hit and control a ball, the more problems you'll give your opponents.

Dear Mr. Country Club Tennis Pro,

Don't you think that my forehand has really improved this year?

Signed,
Nancy Titlewitz

Dear Nancy,

Besides your incredibly late contact with the ball; your loose, floppy, uncontrolled wrist; your annoying tendency to hold the racquet with the wrong grip; your body being spasmodically out of balance; and your strange habit of jumping up and away from the shot itself – I think it's really starting to come around!

156

"I have a $40,000 forehand and an 11-cent backhand."

– Alan King

Unlike the great Alan King, my backhand has always been my best shot. While many of the top players I knew and played against growing up tried to emulate the great two-handed backhands of Bjorn Borg and Jimmy Connors, I always admired and felt more comfortable with the one-handed backhands of players like Ivan Lendl and John McEnroe. Maybe it was all those hours against the backboard. A one-hander just seemed easier to hit. While most advanced players "run around their backhands" when they play, attempting to hit as many forehands as possible, I always do the opposite, a strategy that is often confusing for the majority of my opponents. I can do anything on my backhand side – hit for power, hit for control, change pace, topspin, flat, slice, lob, drop shot, you name it – it was always my best side.

157

This is what makes me so tough to play. Most tennis instruction books will tell you that when you come to net, come into your opponent's backhand, because this is usually the weaker side. But if you employ this strategy against me, you'll usually lose. By the time the majority of my opponents realize that my backhand is my strength, they are typically down 6 - 0, 4 - 1 in a best two out of three set match.

This characteristic of my tennis game points to one of the most important match strategies: playing to your strength as a player is just as important as playing to your opponent's weakness.

Some of my students have hinted to me that they'd prefer it if I talk a little bit less during our lessons together

And Now For Some Backhand From the Best Friend

158

(Who wishes to remain anonymous. Can you blame him?)

I was a college tennis player and, at one time, ranked fourth in Texas. I used to play a couple times a week with the tennis pro who preceded Dan at our club. I generally played to get a workout. Dan's predecessor always gave me a good workout and was relatively non-talkative.

When he left I decided to give Dan a "go." So I set up a game. When I arrived, Dan was already on the court. The second I reached the court Dan started talking very quickly – in his mind, he was cracking jokes. I didn't know what to make of him. Either he was trying to be funny, or the club had hired a lunatic. When we began to play I noticed two things: his tennis strokes were unusual, but he was very consistent. We played a baseline game (no serving), and our points lasted a long time; I got a good workout. Tennis points would end, and Dan would begin talking again.

"I might be better off using a ball machine," I thought to myself after that first match. "The balls come back steady like they come back from Dan, but I'd probably enjoy the company of the machine more than I would enjoy the company of Dan."

I continued to pay Dan for my workouts and, I could hardly believe it, I actually began to understand his sense of humor and realized he wasn't a complete lunatic. I actually started looking forward to these workouts. To this day, Dan and I still play several times a week. Dan improvises his humor and I pretty much play the straight man and insult him continuously for the hour or hour-and-a-half that we are together. We both seem to like it.

159

One pivotal moment in Dan Waintrup's life in which I played a supporting role, concerned the termination of his employment at the club. The General Manager of the club had been looking for any excuse to fire Dan because as silly and unruly as Dan was, the GM was the complete opposite. He didn't appreciate nor could he see the value in Dan's ability to form great relationships with the members of the club.

Dan called my office in a panic one afternoon and told me he was being fired from the country club. After eight years, this really disappointed me because I enjoyed working out with him. I told Dan, "Don't worry, I know most of the members on the board; I am the biggest tennis supporter at the club. I'll make a few calls and straighten everything out. Don't you worry about a thing…I've got connections…I'll take care of this situation…It's who you know in this world, buddy…"

Later that day, I called Dan and he asked excitedly, "How'd it go? I'm back in, right? Did you convince them?"

"You're @#$%&ed," I told him. "You may want to take a look at the Yellow Pages."

After he stopped crying, I made it clear to Dan that, even though his life now was basically destroyed, I still expected him to play with me next week at some other club.

"I still need to get my weekly workout," I told him.

That's the first time I can ever remember Dan giving me the finger.

"Tennis is not a matter of life and death. It's more important than that."

– David Dinkins

Dear Mr. Country Club Tennis Pro,

I was just curious. Are there any other reasons an individual would take a lesson from you besides your obviously superior instructional ability?

Signed,
Sol Soloman

Dear Sol,

It's funny you should ask. It's actually pretty amazing how many other reasons people here at the country club have given me to be on court with this tennis professional:

"I was bored and I had nothing better to do."

"It's raining outside and the golf course is closed."

"This is a great way to work off my hangover."

"The ball machine was broken."

"My doctor said if I don't exercise, I won't live to be fifty."

"I couldn't get anyone else to play with me."

"Even though I didn't feel like coming, I know you'd charge me if I didn't."

cont.

161

"It's cheaper than going to a shrink." ("I know that you'll hit the ball right at me and make me look good," or "I know you'll tell me how great I am, or how great I'm going to be, even if it's not true.")

"I feel bad for you; I know you need the business."

162

Dear Mr. Country Club Tennis Pro,

If you had to name the single most important thing for me to remember when hitting my backhand, what would it be?

Signed,
Libby Lipshitz

Dear Libby,

Drawing on all the knowledge and experience that I've gained in my years as a country club tennis teaching professional, and in reviewing the many hours of hard work we've put in together, it's my opinion that the key to your backhand is to hit your forehand whenever possible!

"The only good backhand I ever ran into was my mother's. She used it across my face."

– Alan King

"My favorite photo! Me and 'The Donald'
chilling in our tuxes in Palm Beach."

#16.

"The demands and long grueling hours teaching
at the country club have sometimes caused me to
do things that I am not very proud of."

"There's nothing like a country club tennis mixed
doubles round robin!"

6. Game, Set, Tree

Dear Mr. Country Club
Tennis Pro,

When they write your
epitaph, what will it be?

Signed,
Stephanie

Dear Stephanie,

Isn't it obvious?
Daniel I. Waintrup
(1956-); R.I.P.
"He had a lot of balls."

An Exercise in Values Clarification

"Come on, come on, you're late again!" I yelled at myself as I drove my prized Volvo convertible down the driveway and out onto the main road. "I cannot be late for the big charity event at the country club tonight," I thought as I floored it down the residential street. "Let's see, did I forget anything?" My mind went through the usual checklist. I always seemed to forget something... Tuxedo, cuff links... I accelerated as I drove toward the expressway. Just then, the phone rang. Going for it, I knocked it on the floor. That could have been my boss or Debby, the event sponsor. "Damn it!" I screamed.

I reached down for the still-ringing phone but it had fallen under the passenger seat. I frantically felt around on the floor for it, taking my eyes off the road for what only seemed like a few seconds. "Got it!" I yelled triumphantly. "Hello, Debby, is everything all set for tonight?" Before I could get an answer, I was startled to see the van in front of me screech to a sudden stop. I swerved to avoid it, probably saving the driver's life, but now I was heading toward a big, fat oak tree at 50 mph. I slammed on the brakes, but not in time to avoid the.......... IMPACT!

Now, it should be pointed out that when you hit a large, immovable object, while driving in a car at a high velocity, without a seat belt, you will be thrown from the vehicle and will very likely kill yourself.

I woke up lying on the side of the road and concluded, after a few exploratory moments, I was not dead. I knew, however, that I was bleeding badly and that my leg hurt an awful lot. I remember thinking, "I'm not sure what hurts more, destroying my beautiful convertible, the incredible pain in my leg, or the fact that it was actually my ex-wife who was calling me on the phone!"

Either way, I had a sinking feeling that I wouldn't be attending the gala that evening, and I certainly wasn't going to be playing in the club championships in a few days.

Even after hitting the tree and nearly killing myself, I was still having some difficulty grasping the severity of the situation, something the emergency crew, thank goodness, was not.

169

"Keep your head perfectly still, sir. DO NOT MOVE! You hear what I'm saying to you?" the big, burly paramedic yelled out. "Mary, get that stretcher over here now!"

"Hey, man, I'm alright. I gotta get up, I gotta get to the to the club…"

"I said DON'T MOVE! You understand English? Tony, bring me my cutting shears, we're going to have to slice off his jacket to get the neck brace on and…"

A jolt went through my body; I couldn't believe my ears!

"Hey, what the hell are you doing? Are you out of you're friggin' mind?" I yelled at the paramedic as he began cutting his way through my new Zegna jacket.

"Stay still, sir, there's no way we can get the brace on and the IV in your arm if you're going to…"

"Listen, buddy," I interrupted, "this jacket is worth more than you make in a month. Put those goddamn scissors away or I'll sue your ugly @#$%&* in court!"

It was good to see that I still had my priorities straight. So what if I almost just killed myself in a serious car accident, was lying on the ground semi-conscious, and was bleeding profusely? How could this idiot think it was okay to ruin my Zegna jacket?! Fortunately for me, the paramedic ignored my pleas, slicing the jacket in two so he could put the neck brace on and the IV in my arm. I cried as I watched its crumpled remains hit the ground.

"How many fingers am I holding up, sir? Can you see my hand? Can you focus in on…"

"Get your hand out of my face! Hey, don't touch that! Who's going to get the stuff out of my car?" I bellowed as the police and rescue crews rummaged through my crumpled vehicle.

"I've got my Rolex and my tux in that car! I want all that @#$%&* back!"

(Hey, I may have almost killed myself, but I still knew what was important; a Rolex is a Rolex!)

"Don't worry, sir, you'll get it all back, I promise," the policeman tried to assure me, probably wondering to himself if he'd ever met an individual whose priorities were more screwed up!

Convinced that I wasn't going to lose any of my precious belongings, I let the emergency personnel load me into the ambulance. But, as we sped towards the hospital, a new concern entered my mind.

"Hey, man, how's my face? Am I all cut up? Am I bleeding real bad?" I quizzed the medic over the sounds of a blaring siren.

In retrospect, it wasn't surprising that I would be concerned with potential scars. After all, in my country club life, with the constant parties, charity events, and the celebrities I got the chance to meet, would I still get that opportunity if I had a disfiguring scar on my face? My thoughts drifted back to just the previous week, when I had the chance to meet Donald Trump at a charity event. Would Mr. Trump have stopped to talk to me if I looked like Frankenstein's brother, or would he have said, "You're fired!"

171

The Donald strutted into the cocktail party with another of those amazingly beautiful women he always seems to be with. The crowd parted like the Red Sea, most people in awe, afraid to say a word to him. But not me – not Dan Waintrup. If I had a chance to meet someone famous, I always took a shot. I lived for these moments.

"Hey Mr. Trump, nice to meet you – Dan Waintrup. How are you?"

"Yeah, how you doing, have we met before?" The Donald said, sounding bored as his eyes scanned the room, looking for a quick way out of the conversation.

"No, sir, we haven't met, but every year I see you at the US Open Tennis Finals in New York. Great match this year, huh?"

"Oh sure, great final this year, kid, great final," The Donald intoned, sounding a little more interested. (Every year, one of the highlights of the US Open men's or women's singles final is to try and guess which of Mr. Trump's ex-wives, girlfriends, children, or movie-star friends are trying to suck up to him in his luxury box – the one right next to the CBS booth.)

"Yeah," I continued, "Sampras played a helluva match, didn't he? Hey, remember right before match point when some idiot in the third deck screamed out in front of 20,000 people, 'Hey, Donald, WHO'S THE BLONDE?' And you turned bright red?"

The Donald laughed. "Jesus – do I remember that, and so did my girlfriend. Hey, you're pretty funny, let's get a picture together!" (See photograph #15, pg. 164.)

As the ambulance sped toward its destination, I thought back to my favorite picture, Donald Trump and me, chilling in our tuxes. A picture I thought would impress my friends and be great for business. Of course, what seemed like a reasonable assumption never quite became a reality. When that picture made the local newspaper my ex-wife was quick to call.

"If you can hang out with Donald Trump, you can pay me more child support!"

Sometimes you just can't win.

I was jolted out of my daydreams as I arrived at the hospital and was quickly wheeled into the emergency room. After several rounds of x-rays, the doctors confirmed my worst fears. I had broken my leg; I wouldn't be playing tennis for a really long time.

As I lay on the stretcher, feeling sorry for myself, nurses scurrying around, my daughter suddenly appeared. I was so relieved to see her.

"Honey, don't worry, I know it looks bad, but the doctor said that…"

"Dad, can I borrow $40?"

"What?"

"You know, I left my wallet at home, and I have to pay for parking in the lot and I've got that concert tonight…"

"Yeah, sure." I woozily collected my thoughts. "I think it's in the bag with my clothes over here… Yeah, that's it, right next to the bloody shirt!"

"Thanks, Dad, you're the greatest. I'll call you later. Hope you're feeling better!"

I remember thinking, "If I were in a coma, would that have made any difference?!"

Either way, it was a long road to recovery. But I had great care and the best nurses around. They were so attentive; all I had to do was ring a bell and there would be someone to take care of me within thirty seconds, day or night.

Can you just imagine if you tried this at home?

"Honey, it's so great to be home; the nurses were fantastic. They gave me this bell so anytime I need something from you I can just ring it and…"

"They gave you a what?"

"They gave me a bell. You know, when I need new bandages, or some ice, or a drink, I can just ring…"

"Let me tell you something, buster, you better not be ringing a bell in this house."

"But, pumpkin, if I need something, I can just ring it and you'll be able to…"

"Listen, bud, let's get one thing straight. This Jewish woman is not ever going to come running when you ring a bell. Don't even think about it. You ring that bell once and you'll be sleeping in the cabana! Remember that colonoscopy you had last year? Well, you'll need to get another one because that's where they're going to find that bell!"

I thought long before I replied, "Well, can I call you on the intercom?"

Dear Mr. Country Club Tennis Pro,

Do you ever teach tennis on the Jewish holidays?

Signed,
Theresa Weiner

Dear Theresa,

Well, I try not to teach tennis on any of the Jewish holidays. (You know, what would the old man think?) But if I do, I try to get into the spirit. For example, on Passover I've been heard to say when working with a student: "For godsakes, Mrs. Lebowitz, you've got to run to the ball. Get those matzah balls moving. The Seder's going to start without you, bubby!"

"The reason the pro says to keep your head down is so you can't see him laughing."

– Phyllis Diller

Waintrup's Rules for Winning
Hit! Then Look

You've taken hundreds of lessons on your topspin forehand. You know where every muscle of your body, where every inch of your racquet should be before, during, and after the stroke. Your tennis teacher has been happy to give you this knowledge because it helps him make the payments on his new Porsche. But there's a problem. When it comes to making the shot in a match, when it comes to executing the shot under pressure, you continually miss it. This is beginning to drive you crazy. You often fantasize about dropping your pro's Porsche in the river — with him in it!

Why do you keep missing this — or any other shot under pressure? Is there anything that can be done? If you were a truly advanced player, you would understand that having the technical knowledge of how to hit a particular shot is not enough. All the top players know that their ability to continually hit a shot when it counts depends largely on how tough they are mentally and how disciplined they are during the tennis stroke.

Good players know that controlling the ball in tennis, assuming you know what kind of stroke you're hitting, depends on how stationary you can keep your eyes and head before, during, and after contact has been made. To achieve this balance, this important discipline so necessary at impact, imagine your eyes taking a picture of the contact point. Your eyes are the camera, and the contact point of the stroke your intended picture. Move your eyes or jerk your head during a groundstroke and the picture will become out of focus. Move your eyes or jerk your head while you're hitting a tennis ball and your shot will usually end up in Buffalo!

So remember, stay under mental and physical control during your groundstrokes. Take those nice, clear pictures of contact and watch your consistency improve. Who knows, maybe someday you'll be driving the Porsche! (See photograph #9, pg. 74.)

Dear Mr. Country Club Tennis Pro,

I remember how they use to talk about the great Bjorn Borg in his prime, and how it used to be said that the only way one could ever beat him was to "Hit the shot of your life and come to net." Is that how it is if I were to play you?

Signed,
Charlotte Fineman

Dear Charlotte,

Well Charlotte, the concepts are somewhat similar, although if you were playing me at this point in my career – an old, overweight, out-of-shape country club teaching professional – the saying that might be more applicable would be, "Hit an average approach shot, and wait for the mistake!"

Dear Mr. Country Club Tennis Pro,

I know you had that horrible car accident last year and injured your leg pretty bad. Does it hurt when you play?

Signed,
Rebecca

Dear Rebecca,

Only when I'm losing.

Dear Mr. Country Club Tennis Pro,

I know the key to playing a good tennis match is to stay positive and in control of yourself when you're on court. Unfortunately, I have a terrible temper and it's often extremely difficult for me to accomplish this after a few bad shots. Is there anything I can look for that will tell me if I'm getting a little too negative, and thus, ineffective, during a match?

Signed,
Howie Blumberg

Dear Howie,

You know you're probably getting a little out of control during a match when:

1) You hear people walking by your court during the match wondering out loud, "Is there some other brother in the McEnroe family playing tennis right now who we haven't heard of?"

2) You're still in the first set and you've already broken three racquets.

3) You hit a great first serve and scream at yourself, "You stink!"

4) You hit the best topspin lob winner of your life and congratulate yourself with, "You're the worst player of all time!"

5) You're yelling obscenities so loud that after the match, a club member comes up to you and blames you for the triple bogey he had on the 16th hole, 200 yards from the court you played on.

6) Every time your opponent hits a great shot, he has to duck immediately or risk being hit by a flying tennis ball or racquet.

7) You find yourself bleeding from more than five places on your body from all the times you've been diving for balls you have little chance of returning.

Dear Mr. Country Club Tennis Pro,

I know that as a country club tennis teaching professional you have to have an incredible amount of patience, but have there ever been times when even you couldn't wait for the lesson to end?

Signed,
Molly

Dear Molly,

Of course! There have been many times I wasn't overly enamored with the individual I was teaching. I remember the time I had a playing lesson with a pretty good player, who happened to be a psychotherapist. Upon missing a forehand during a rally, he told me that, in his professional opinion, errors like this were often due to one's inability to relate to his or her mother on an intimate level. I said, "Hmmm, very interesting." After double faulting on one of my service games, he was certain that I obviously had been suppressing an enormous amount of hostility towards my father. I thought to myself, "How many years could I actually get for assaulting one of my students?" Fortunately, I chose to respond in a less violent manner. After he missed a backhand, I told him he had probably missed the shot because he sucked!

cont.

180

Another time, I was teaching a woman who I thought was having a bad day, but later found out was really suffering from PMS.

I started off the hour by cheerfully saying, "Hi, I'm Dan Waintrup, the teaching pro here, what would you like to work on today?" She said, "Go to hell!" Regaining my composure, I suggested, "Well, maybe you'd like to rally a few backhands?" She told me what I could do with my backhands, but I won't repeat it here. After an hour with this woman, the psychotherapist didn't seem so bad!

I've been able to maintain my reputation as one of the best and most knowledgable country club teaching professionals around by using my time off court to improve myself in every way possible

The Shrink's Notebook

4/10 –

Patient is 38 yo WM w/ no history of mental disorders. Mental state examination is unremarkable. No risks to self or others identified.

Patient is recently divorced; has 2 children, children reside with mother, normal relations

Patient is college graduate now working as country club tennis pro

Patient claims to be depressed and having conflicts with his boss "he wants to control my life" and ex-wife "she wants to control my life"

P is youngest child of 3 – the baby and the only boy (spoiled rotten?)

P is son of rabbi and manifests predictable competitivness, needs to be the center of attention – odd references to stolen Bar Mitzvah money??

Attempts to explore relationship with mother reveal nothing unusual "she wants to control my life" – typical acts of rebellion

P feels he is dead-ended in career, marriage failed, financial frustrations, typical child visitation conflicts with ex-wife

P says he needs new career, needs to make more money, needs a new car = mild depression; anxiety appears to be about the present rather than the future; does not appear P thinks beyond the day after tomorrow.

......This guy is a spoiled party-boy, fails to acknowledge causal relationship between his lack of focus and lack of accomplishment, refuses to grow up, maturity issues; self-absorbed......

Inquiry as to his goals he responds, "I want a Mercedes convertible, a huge house, a beautiful wife, and I want to travel the world."

......Christ, he doesn't know the difference between a goal and a fantasy – "I would like to play with Bruce Springsteen, live on a sailboat in Fiji, and be married to Miss August 2003"......stop for soy milk and Pampers on the way home......

183

......Yawn......Maybe I should work on my tennis game......Yawn......

5/23 –

Patient arrives aggitated following a conflict with general manager who thinks he's getting a little too friendly with some of the members; GM is not as popular with members as patient

P teaches tennis lessons on call at club and often parties with members and friends in the evenings

......He gets paid to be a tennis bum, hang out with rich guys and party with their wives; they pay him to do this and he's complaining?......

P is unhappy at his current salary level and doesn't feel he can live the lifestyle he deserves, obsessed with the trappings of wealth

......"lifestyle he deserves" – give me a break......This guy has never worked a day in his life......

P is balding......Perceive envy of my ponytail

P says he can't take the pressure of this level of physical exhertion much longer, has physical symptoms – loss of voice from too much screaming, bad knees, weak back

......This guy is starting to get on my nerves......He should try a caseload of whacko fruitcakes 8 or 10 hours a day......He should try dealing with the @#$%& health insurance companies......Book tennis lesson with pro at gym......

9/15 –

P arrives agitated because of a conflict with his mother; particular anger because mother wants to send raincoat?; parents frequently suggest P should go to business school and get a real job. P is resistant

......Still rebelling and he's almost 40......

184

P says he couldn't make it in an academic setting at this point in his life, plus evening classes would interfere with his social life. P hasn't read a book "in a few years" – "Does *Sports Illustrated* count?" P doesn't own and cannot use a computer.

......Give me a friggin' break......Where has this guy been?......Detect envy of my docking station and 17" flat panel screen monitor......Bring Palm to next appointment......

P indicates he sometimes has difficulty focusing at 7 a.m. lessons, especially after only 2 hours of sleep and who knows how much "Jackie D" the night before

......Possible attention deficit disorder......When I asked if anyone in his family had ever been diagnosed with AD/HD he responded, "Not me, pal, I always use protection."......

Asked P if he did well in school, he replied, "I did a lot better than most guys. I had a date pretty much every weekend." Good grades? "Decent." Did you like school? "It was okay; lunch was good and I was the top-ranked varsity player on the tennis team. I had a really hot French teacher."

P indicates he has explored other career options such as real estate, but he was not successful. "People just didn't want to list their houses with me. I don't get it. Even my best friend. When you list a property you don't really have to do anything after you put the sign in the yard. I thought this was the job for me."

......P is highly delusional about work......Oh, brother, I don't know if can get through another session with this guy griping about his life......But at $150/hour......Boat payment due on Friday......

11/11 –

Patient arrives agitated because he's been single for 4 months and he hasn't met a woman who "really does it for me"; says there are many attractive women in the world but none of them have exactly the portfolio he's looking for......

......Freud would have a field day with this guy...... Authority figures, plays with balls, hangs out in locker rooms all day, women with "bodacious ta-tas"......Look for article in past issue of *Mental Health Practitioner* on developmental disabilities in adult males......

P went to Las Vegas with best friend over holiday weekend; can't remember anything after noon on Saturday; but he knows he was at the Mirage 'cause he has a credit card receipt from the bar – "Must have bought a round for the whole casino!" Ha ha......

.......Possible bipolar diagnosis; when asked if he feels he may experience mood swings, he said, "Yeah, especially after a box of Butterscotch Tastykakes and a large Dr. Brown's Cream Soda."

Asked P to describe what happens when he is depressed – says he feels like life has no meaning, nobody understands him, he knows he could be a millionaire if everyone would just get out of his way, he was meant to play the world tour and these other guys just got in the way, he had it nailed, "I could beat anybody in my college days, I was 'The Wall.'"

This guy gives new meaning to the term "pompous ass"......

Personal Note: Don't' forget six-pack of Red Bull and No-Doz tablets for his appointment!

6/10 –

Patient cancels appoint; hospitalized after car accident

8/20 –

Patient fails to show up for appointment; left voice mail: "My physical therapist had a last minute cancellation and was able to squeeze me in; Doc, these Swedish girls really know how to use their hands"......Bill patient at 50% for failing to cancel 24 hours in advance

9/2 –

Patient arrives agitated due to fears that leg injury will preclude him from resuming his teaching career, extreme anxiety over making child support payments on the 15th; sick of eating at McDonald's; conflict with general manager at club accelerates; ex-wife called twice on cell phone during session.

......Patient seems to be on crash course......Cha-ching, Cha-ching......Take Jaguar in for oil change

4/28 –

Patient cancels appointment; says he has been terminated from country club and needs some time to pull himself together

6/12 –

Patient leaves after 15 min; says he has met the woman of his dreams; must run to catch a plane to go shopping for antiques in Paris; "Was that you in the Red Sox owner's box at the game the other night? Guess not. Ciao, bubby!"

......I never really liked this guy......CASE CLOSED.

188

"My father was ecstatic when I
finally got my MBA."

"Up to this point in my life, everything's coming up roses."

Jay O'Brien

"The Wall" and the wall that played such
a major role is his development as a tennis
player, enjoy an emotional reunion.

7. 40, Love –
Advantage Mr. Waintrup

"You either go to bed with someone or you play tennis with them. But don't do both."

– Art Buchwald

Finally Getting Good at Doubles

I met the beautiful woman who is now my wife – where else? – on the tennis court. I was teaching a clinic at the club and during a drill I noticed one of the participants was in tears and had run off the court. Fearing that I had offended her in some way, I ran after her and followed her to the members' lounge. When I got there I noticed her sitting in the corner, weeping and very distraught. I approached her to see if she was alright. In our subsequent conversation, I found out that she had just gotten divorced and was a little depressed.

"Well," I thought to myself, "maybe I'll just tell her a little story and try to cheer her up."

I had noticed this woman around the club and found her very attractive. Now that I knew she was single, it was time to make an impression.

"You think you got problems? Let me tell you about my little visit to the proctologist yesterday." (What a pick-up line. Am I smooth or what?)

"Excuse me?" she asked, looking up at me a little incredulously.

"Yeah, well anyway, I had to get this flexible sigmoidoscopy. Ever had one? Painful as hell! I'm still walking funny."

"Uhhh…" She looked around the room, maybe not quite believing what she was hearing.

"Anyway, this sadistic pig – I mean doctor – is intent on having a conversation with me as he's, you know, placing this tube up where the sun don't shine. You know what I mean? I couldn't believe it."

"No way!" My future wife started laughing a little nervously.

"'So, how are the kids?' the doctor asks."

"AHHHHH! Damn that hurts! What did you say? Great – just great."

"Great weather we're having, huh?"

"Owwwwww! What? Oh, sure, great weather. Is this going too take long?"

"Oh, not too long. Hey, how about those Red Sox, huh?"

"Jesus! Oh, yeah, they're playing great. I can't breathe…"

"I'm more of a football fan myself. You go to any Patriots games this year?"

"What? Yeah, whatever! I like football – please finish! The cramps!"

"How about basketball? Do you think the Celtics have a chance at the playoffs?"

"Help meeeeeeeee!"

"I'm lying there in excruciating pain and this guy's talking to me like nothing's going on, like he's my best friend. Unbelievable!"

My student and future wife was no longer depressed – she was laughing too hard. One thing led to another and the rest is history.

Fortunately for me, my wife is a very forgiving person. I found this out on our wedding night. It had been an amazingly stressful couple of days. All of our friends and relatives were in town. There were a million things to do, a million little details that had to be taken care of.

Maybe I started getting a little stressed out when Linda and I had this conversation a few hours before our impending nuptials:

"So, honey, I never even thought to ask because we've been so busy. What are we serving at the reception?"

"Oh, it's going to be great. You'll love it – don't worry about it."

"Well, darling, I'm sure I'll love it, but I was just curious. You know my parents and most of their relatives are kosher."

"Well, we're starting off with lobster."

"Excuse me?"

"Lobster – it's your favorite! Is there a problem?"

"Sweetheart, my father's a @#$%& rabbi. You know he can't eat shellfish!"

"Well, it's too late to change the menu now. He won't even notice. Don't be such a worry wart."

"Jesus! What else?"

"Shrimp…"

"WHAT!?"

"You love shrimp! And caviar, the finest Beluga…"

(I'm hyperventilating! I think I'm going to have a heart attack!)

"Is there anything he can eat?"

"I have a lovely challah. He likes bread, doesn't he?"

"Oy @#$%& vey!"

As we stood under the *chuppah*, I tried not to think about what my father's reaction would be when he found out what food was being served at the reception. Of course, this was a little difficult to do since he was standing five feet in front of me performing my wedding. (I wondered, would the world be witness to the first instance of a rabbi having a seizure at his own son's wedding?)

Linda and I were both extremely nervous and asked my father to keep the sermon as short as possible.

"Please, Dad, promise me. Ten minutes, max. Alright?" I begged him in private, as we signed the *ketubah* (marriage contract) before we began.

"Son, don't worry. It'll be over when it's over."

"That's what I'm afraid of."

"I'll do the best that I can. You don't want to rush such a blessed occasion."

Over the years, my father had always had a little problem being succinct during his sermons on very momentous occasions. Maybe it was because he just loved being on the pulpit, being on a stage, performing in front of a crowd.

Growing up, I used to be the usher at all of my father's Friday night services. I would stand in the back and he would signal me at the proper time to let in the late-arriving congregants. Over time, as I got older, I would signal him when I thought his sermons were running a little too long.

196

"Remember that signal I used to give you when you were getting a little too verbose up on the pulpit, Dad? You know, the 'cut it, cut it' sign? The hand crossing under the throat? I'll do that today if I think you're running a little long. Keep it short and sweet, okay?"

The Rabbi only smiled.

I knew he was up to something. I just couldn't figure out what. Linda and I were so nervous we were practically hanging onto each other for dear life. As I was thinking about how relieved I would be when the ceremony was over, I heard these ominous words:

"And now I'd like to say a few words about my son, Daniel, and his beloved bride."

This is what I had feared most. I glanced at my watch and was astonished to realize that the service had already been going on for twenty minutes, and my father hadn't even begun his little speech yet.

"Short and sweet. Keep it short and sweet," I whispered forcefully, knowing in my heart it probably wasn't going to make any difference what I said to the Rabbi at this point.

And then came the words that I'll very likely remember for the rest of my life:

"You know, dear friends, marriage is like a cake."

"Oh no, Dad, don't go there. Please, don't go there," I remember thinking to myself.

"If a marriage is to be a truly successful partnership, the husband and wife must understand and believe in the ingredients of the cake."

I felt my bride start to shake. I'm thinking she's about to faint.

"In this cake are what I like to call the 'raisins of responsibility,' which represent the respect and commitment brides and grooms must have for each other if their marriage is going to succeed."

My knees started feeling a little weak and sweat began forming on my brow.

"Of course, in every cake you must have flour – the 'flour of fortitude.' Each partner must have the strength, the courage, the fortitude, and the determination to believe in the sanctity of their partnership."

I can't take it anymore. I try giving my father the sign. "That's it! Time to wrap it up. Put the glass beneath my foot, Rabbi. I'm ready to end the ceremony – please!"

But it's too late. Once my father has the stage, once my father has a theme, there's no stopping him. With each additional ingredient of the marriage cake, I feel my wife's nails digging deeper and deeper into my arm. I am certain she is going to rip a few holes in my tux and start drawing blood.

198

Finally, my father finishes.

"*Mazel Tov!* Congratulations! Let the party begin," everyone cried out. And what a party it was. The rabbi didn't say a word about the food. To this day, I'm not certain if he was too drunk, or in a state of shock! Either way, it was a grand celebration for us – for everyone – both our families and all our friends.

The other thing that was weighing heavily on my mind as the reception progressed was the best man's toast. Now my best man – you've actually heard from him earlier in this opus – and I had some pretty wild times together, both on and off the court. I knew that my buddy had prepared some written remarks and, although I was honored and impressed by his preparatory diligence, it occurred to me that maybe I should take a glance at his remarks prior

to their public recitation. It was a fortuitous thing that I
requested the once-over.

He reluctantly handed me his notes. I read the first
scrawled line and almost had a heart attack. What he
had written was not only incriminating, but it absolutely
could not be publicly discussed in front of my family and
friends. What was he thinking?

"No, you can't say that. And you definitely can't say that.
Let's see… Oh, yeah! I remember that night! Billy, how
many times do I have to tell you? What happens in Vegas
stays in Vegas! This @#$%&* comes out or I won't
make it to my wedding night!"

By the time I had read through all of his notes, my
buddy's speech was in 5,000 little pieces, and I made
him swear under penalty of death that none of these
stories would ever see the light of day. My best man was
incensed. He had been rather proud of his prepared
remarks and envisioned himself as the comedic tour de
force. Now he had about sixty seconds to come up with
some new material.

199

My buddy was to offer his toast after my father and
another rabbi had done their blessings. He was at such a
loss for material that after they had cut the bread he said,
"How do I follow that, two old Jews cutting bread?"

The silence that followed the remark was deafening. It
is something I'll not soon forget. After this bomb, he ad-
libbed some benign pleasantries but never really regained
his footing. He has never forgiven me for yanking his

hilarious script and to this day threatens to resurrect it at other ceremonious events – like on my fiftieth birthday. I expect he will get back at me for this one someday. If you're in the audience when he lets loose, remember you read it here first.

After what had been a very long, yet gloriously magical day, we finally went upstairs. We were in the honeymoon suite at the Ritz with an icy bottle of Dom. I stripped out of my tux, and lay down on the luscious Egyptian cotton sheets. Linda stepped into the dressing room to put on something sexy for our wedding night. A few minutes later she slides into our marital bed and was greeted by the loud, vociferous, earth-shattering snoring of her new husband. I had passed out from sheer mental and physical exhaustion.

That was the first time I found out what a very forgiving person my wife really is. Fortunately for me, it wouldn't be the last. I experienced this wonderful quality of my wife's personality yet again a few years later on one of our frequent trips to Vermont.

We were having this wonderfully romantic dinner at some beautiful resort in the mountains and beginning our second bottle of Groth Cabernet.

The evening could not have been going better, but then the trouble began.

"What do you think we should do for our anniversary this year, darling?" my wife began, gazing at me coyly.

"Oh, I don't know. We could go to New York and see a show, or Vegas, or maybe Napa might be nice this year. Whatever you want, dear."

Even in my increasingly inebriated state, I sensed there was something behind this question, I just couldn't figure out what. My wife loves exploiting the mental block I seemed to have when it comes to remembering important dates like birthdays or anniversaries. She enjoys testing me on this knowledge, preferably after a couple of glasses of wine. My worst fears were realized.

"By the way, what is the date of our anniversary, sweetheart?"

"Damn it," I muttered to myself. I knew she was up to something. I could never remember the exact date of our wedding, a topic my therapist loved discussing.

"Well, it's in June, of course. I know when it is," I shot back defensively, hoping she would get too intoxicated to continue this line of questioning.

"When in June? What's the exact date, sweetheart?" she insisted, a little more of an edge in her voice, as she poured me yet another glass of wine.

"Oh, darling, please. Of course I know the date. It's insulting you would even ask such a question. Excuse me. I'll be right back. I need to go to the men's room." And with that I quickly got up from the table and started to walk to the downstairs bathroom trying to figure out how in the hell I was going to remember when our anniversary was, or find someone who could help me out.

"Think, think, you idiot," I berated myself. "Who can I call who would know? I've got it! My mother! I'll call my mother. She was there; she has to remember."

My cell phone wasn't working, so I found a pay phone.

"Hello, Mom. Yeah, everything's fine. No, I didn't get the raincoat you sent me. I've told you before, I've got ten raincoats. Don't send me a raincoat. Listen, when was I married? Not the first time – to Linda. I know I should know the date! How can you not remember? Ask Dad. What do you mean he can't remember? He performed the ceremony! Jesus! Call my sister and have her leave a message on my voicemail. I gotta go back upstairs. I can't stall much longer."

I hung up the phone and hurried upstairs; my wife sensed something was wrong.

"Are you okay?" she asked. "You look a little tense."

"Yeah, I think the foie gras didn't agree with me. I'm having cramps. Ugghhh. I better get down to the men's room again. Be right back – promise."

I didn't wait for her response and rushed back downstairs to the pay phone.

Unfortunately, the restaurant only had one phone, and, naturally, one of the busboys was on it.

"Hey, man, please, I need the phone. You gotta get off now!" I pleaded. "I'm a cardiac surgeon at Mass General and it's a matter of life and death."

"Hey, listen, I'm talking to my girlfriend. @#$%&* you. You're just going to have to wait."

I was getting desperate. I was willing to do anything.

"Alright. How much? How much to get off? Come on – give me a price."

"A price? You want a price? Let's see… Fifty bucks?"

"What? Are you out of your @#$%&* mind? To make one call?"

203

"Listen, buddy, you can afford it. I saw the bottles of wine you were ordering. Pay up."

"Goddamn mercenary," I muttered as I handed over the cash. I had no choice. I had to get that information.

I called my voicemail and got the date. "Of course, June 23! Why do I have such trouble remembering that? Thank God for my sister," I thought to myself as I sprinted upstairs with the knowledge that I was certain would help me avert a marital crisis.

But as I approached our table, I saw the waitress talking to my wife and, as I got closer, heard her remark, "You know I was downstairs earlier and overheard your husband talking to his mother. It sounded like they were having such a nice conversation. I wish my son would call me more often."

"Oy @#$%&*ing vey," I thought as I sat down.

"So you called your mommy? Isn't that nice? What did you talk about?" my wife asked with a devilish grin.

"Goddamn waitress," I lamented to myself.

Fortunately for me, my wife was well into the second bottle of Cabernet and was willing to forgive the transgression, but only if I promised never to forget again.

"I promise, I promise! Let's drink some wine. I need to relax. It's been somewhat of a stressful evening!"

Another great example of my wife's ability to forgive and forget was the time last spring when we went to the opening of the ballet. After the show, we attended the traditional party that's always thrown for the trustees, supporters, and performers at one of the area's top hotels. As my wife and I sat in the ballroom of the Ritz, sipping our Dom Perignon and enjoying our Beluga caviar, I couldn't help but notice something eerily familiar about the room. Like I had been there before. You know, that sense of déjà vu.

"Darling, I can't quite place it, but it feels like we've been in this room before. You know what I mean?" I asked innocently, through sips of champagne.

There's probably nothing that could have adequately prepared me for what came next.

"You're right, sweetheart. We have been here before. We were married in this room!"

I remember thinking, "I just hope that when she divorces me, I get to keep the Armani."

Amazingly enough, my beloved once again forgave me for this incredible example of mental ineptitude.

My wife seems to have accepted the fact that I'm a "work in progress." She's accepted the reality that I'm always going to look a little disheveled – "slightly askew" as she likes to call it. But I'm working on it. It's just that, in my new life, it's not always easy remembering that when you go to a black tie event on a June evening in Boston, you must wear the platinum watch with the matching studs and the proper cuff links with the right belt and the correct shoes, which is completely different from attending a black tie event on a February afternoon in Palm Beach, where you must wear the gold watch with the matching studs and the corresponding cuff links with the right color belt and the matching shoes.

205

Got it?

I rarely do!

Of course, the key to any successful marriage is not just to dress correctly, but also be able to communicate honestly and openly about life and whatever problems you need to resolve as a couple. My wife and I like to accomplish this through the many long walks we've been known to take together over the years. One of our neighbors often commented on how wonderful it was to see a couple spending so much time together and communicating so openly and meaningfully.

"I always see the two of you walking together and it looks like you're having such a wonderful time. Joking, laughing, and talking honestly. You're both so very lucky."

I was quick to set her straight.

"Oh yeah, we're communicating openly and honestly. You know what she's saying to me? 'SHUT UP! PLEASE! SHUT THE HELL UP! CAN'T YOU CLOSE THAT BIG MOUTH OF YOURS FOR MORE THAN THIRTY SECONDS? I CAN'T TAKE IT ANYMORE! NEXT TIME I'M BRINGING THE iPOD! JESUS!'"

Sometimes, looks can be deceiving.

"I'm at the age where food has taken the place of sex in my life. In fact, I've just had a mirror put over my kitchen table."

– Rodney Dangerfield

One of the activities that my wife and I do love to do together is eat great food and go to fantastic restaurants. We've been to some of the finest in the world – New York, London, Paris, LA… Ahh, the memories.

And it shows. We're both very happy together, but have gained a little weight enjoying the finest wines and cuisine. She often jokes that the only way either of us is ever going to lose any weight is if we separate or divorce – then we'll be depressed and won't eat!

207

Almost always after having one of these huge, sumptuous meals at one of the finest restaurants in the world, I can barely breathe. The belt buckle on my pants is shouting out "No Mas!" and I swear it feels like I'm about to make history by being the first man to give birth. The only thing I want to do is crawl up into my bed, put my head on my pillow, and forget about the incredible culinary delights I've just engorged myself with for the last four hours.

And, as I stumble into bed, barely able to move or breathe, that's when I can usually count on my beloved turning on the Emeril Lagasse show on the Food Network.

"Now, to make the Osso Bucco correctly, we must place the onions and the potatoes and the carrots…"

"Do we have to listen to that now? I'm about to throw up. Please don't. I can't take it!"

"Shhh – he's about to tell me his favorite recipe. Don't be such a baby!"

"Honey, they're going to have to perform a cesarean on me in two seconds. Please?!"

"Now, for the lamb shank I like to simmer the beef for a few hours, then I add the sauce…"

208

"I'm going to puke. I swear, if you don't turn it off… Honey…"

I guess my wife isn't always that forgiving!

The Big Match

"Show me a good loser, and I'll show you an idiot."

— Leo Durocher (baseball manager)

Every individual who's ever played the game of tennis has a favorite match or set or game that is remembered as a defining moment in his or her competitive career. For the

great Andre Agassi, one of these moments could have
been the Wimbledon Championship he won in 1992.
For my ninety-year-old student, Mo Weinberg, it was
probably the first time we got through a lesson together
without me having to administer CPR.

For this country club tennis teaching professional, it
was the recent match I played in the finals of the Men's
Singles championships at the Palm Beach Country Club.

Unfortunately for my opponent, a friend of mine who
had also been a tennis teaching professional for a number of years, and me, the match took place on one of the
hottest days of the year. The temperature was over 100
degrees, and the humidity was unbearable.

209

We were two overweight and out-of-shape Jewish tennis professionals playing a two out of three set match,
barely being able to move or breathe; it was not a pretty
sight. The tournament director showed his unabashed
confidence in our conditioning and our ability to make it
through the contest alive by parking an ambulance next
to the court. We both wanted to win very badly, but the
heat was unbearable and we were both gasping for air,
barely able to play. It was so hot and suffocating during
the first set that I swear I began to hear voices.

One was my mother.

"Meshuganah! It's too hot to play. Are you trying to kill
yourself? Nothing is worth this aggravation. Have a cold
drink. And don't forget to call me!"

And of course, my ex-wife wasn't going to be ignored.

"If you're going to die on me and your two children, I hope you at least had the decency to increase your life insurance, you selfish bastard."

Despite the incredibly difficult playing conditions, neither of us was going to give up. There was something admirable about two old pros giving 100 percent in the asphyxiating heat, fighting to the death, playing until either one of us might collapse. Unfortunately, despite this noble display of guts and determination, one of the problems that I traditionally had in these highly enervating, highly stressful matches that I played throughout my career was to say something that I would usually regret later on.

Midway through the first set, after the loss of an excruciatingly long point, I screamed out, "Jesus! I can't @#$%&ing breathe!"

"Have your wife give you mouth-to-mouth," one of my friends blurted out from the stands.

"Right, Barry. Give me some motivation here, bubby. How about that beautiful wife of yours, buddy? You know what I mean. That'll get me going! – Oops, oh, sorry, honey! I didn't see you there! Just kidding!"

"Oy @#$%&ing vey!" I thought to myself. Just because I'm about to have a heart attack on a tennis court doesn't mean I have to insult the wife!

Despite the forgiving nature of my better half, my mind drifted off into what most women's reaction might be to such a comment.

"Whew! That was a tough point. Boy, it's hot out here!" I said sitting down between games, taking a sip of Gatorade.

"Yeah, you're playing great, honey," my wife replied detached and unemotionally.

I noticed she was making some notes on a piece of paper.

"What are you writing? The list of who we're having at the dinner party next week?"

"No."

"Some new recipes?"

"Not quite."

"Notes on my match?" I asked facetiously.

"Don't flatter yourself. I'm compiling a list of who my next husband might be. You know, just in case you don't make it through the match."

"What?"

"Well, darling, you've got to be prepared in life. You never know what's going to happen. You look like you might have some kind of seizure out here. A girl's got to be prepared. I hear that lawyer, Stan Grossberg, just got separated. He's a nice guy."

"Do you have to do that now?'

"Oh, darling, don't you mind me! You go play and have a good time. I'll be right here if you need me."

"Yeah, I bet."

Somehow I managed to forget the horror of this day-dream, and played my best tennis in years.

Both of us played our guts out that day, but I somehow managed to beat my friend and fellow teaching pro in a close match. As difficult as conditions were that day, we both managed to raise our level of play and had a terrifically competitive third set. Competing in the final that day reminded me of how great a game tennis can be when you keep a positive attitude and you give 100 percent of yourself mentally and physically. Most importantly, playing in that third set reminded me of what an amazing game tennis is, especially when you compare it to a "sport" like golf.

As the great McEnroe once said, "Is golf really a sport, in all honesty? I thought in a sport you had to run at some point!"

The great tennis pro, commentator, and author Peter Burwash sums it all up this way: "In golf, you miss your first three shots and it ruins your whole day. In tennis, it's just Love – 40."

Waintrup's Rules for Winning
The Art of Winning Well

You've worked long and hard on developing a pretty solid tennis game. You not only have the ability to hit offensively with topspin off your forehand and backhand, but have developed an excellent defensive slice as well. You can come to net, volley, and finish off a long point if you need to, and you've really improved your on-court movement and reaction to your opponent's shots. Your serve has improved dramatically with the addition of being able to hit with varying degrees of spin, speed, and placement during your service games. Your tennis pro has been very happy to work with you and help you attain this high level of knowledge. He just returned from his latest trip to the Caribbean!

213

There is one "small" piece of knowledge that your pro hasn't given you yet, however; he's never taught you how to win.

For every tennis player out there who looks great on a tennis court and has seemingly mastered every facet of the game, it's amazing how many have never mastered the "Art of Winning." These players never learn that if they get too caught up in trying to win the match, too caught up in allowing the particular game or set they are playing to become too important to them, they'll consistently get nervous, choke, and lose.

Every top player knows that the key to winning and performing your best is learning how to relax on a tennis court. These players know that the key to playing at their highest competitive level is to breathe, stay calm, and allow their natural ability to take over. Of course, this is easier said than done. It's certainly no easy task to "let it happen" on a tennis court when you're playing a big match. It's never easy to relax when you're playing in the finals of the club championships and the match is important to you.

In my own experience, I've been able to play my best when I concentrate on just trying to be consistent, on just trying to breathe and react and move my feet and concentrate on making one shot at a time. I've found that I give myself the best chance to perform at my highest competitive level and to win when I don't center on winning, but on being consistent. If you can learn to concentrate on being consistent, on not being so "result-oriented," you're doing everything you can on a tennis court to be successful.

One of the things I've always told myself before a big match that helps me relax and gets me to concentrate on the things I need to think about to perform at my highest level competitively is the following: "I may not win this match, but I know one thing I am going to do, and that's to go out there and react quickly to my opponent's shots and try to be as consistent as I can and make my opponent beat me." I take comfort before a big match in knowing that I can always control a certain aspect of it; I can always control the effort I'm about to give and the fact that I'm going to go out on that tennis court to work hard and move my feet and react and play consistent tennis and give 100 percent. All great players know that if they are doing that, then they are doing all they can as a tennis player, physically and mentally, to perform at the highest competitive level.

Who knows, maybe someday it'll be you taking trips to the Caribbean!

"It's a funny thing about life; if you refuse to accept anything but the very best, you very often get it..."

– W. Somerset Maugham

215

And They Say There's No Justice in the World...

Not surprisingly, my beloved wife maintained her membership at the country club where I had worked and been fired from a few years earlier. And by marrying her, in accordance with the bylaws of the club, I became an automatic member. In essence, as a new member, the General Manager who fired me now worked for me.

I walked into the club the first day after my marriage and encountered the man who had so coldly and unceremoniously ended my country club teaching career.

"How are you today, Mr. Waintrup? It's so good to see you. I hear you've become a new member." My old boss smiled nervously through gritted teeth.

"That's correct. Is my locker ready?"

"Absolutely, sir. Right this way. It'd be my pleasure to show you where it is."

"Excellent. Who's the teaching pro now? I hear we have great service here at the county club."

216

"Only the best for our members. Here we are – locker 327. Is there anything else I can do for you today?"

"Yeah, there is one thing… Who's going to shine my shoes today?"

"I'll make sure that's taken care of, sir."

"You do that," I said with a winning smile.

My old boss walked away with my shoes, probably wishing he had a gun or a hole to crawl into.

And they say there's no justice in the world!

Epilogue:
"You're not just all wet;
You're in Denial!"

Dear Mr. Country Club Tennis Pro,

Every time I come to the club I see you playing sets with opponents who appear much older than you. Am I correct, or are these men actually around the same age as you?

Signed,
Murray Dorfman

Dear Murray,

Actually, you are correct, Murray. I love playing men who are older than me; it makes me feel so much better about myself!

And I Ain't the Only One Who's in Deep

Dear Mr. Country Club Tennis Pro,

I happened to be playing on the court next to you yesterday during one of your lessons and I couldn't believe all the excuses your student was giving you every time he made a mistake. Do you find this happening often here at the country club?

Signed,
Mel Goplewitz

218

Dear Mel,

It's truly amazing how many excuses I've been given for missing a particular shot during a lesson in all my years as a country club teaching professional. I've enclosed a partial list.
"I missed that forehand because":

1) "I had too much to eat last night."
2) "I had too much to drink last night."
3) "I had too much wine last night."
4) "I had too much beer last night."
5) "I had too much wine and vodka last night."
6) "I had too much vodka and beer last night."
7) "I had too much wine, vodka, and beer last night."
8) "I threw up all night."
9) "I'm hungover and threw up all night."
10) "I was out all night with my friends and didn't get any sleep."

cont.

11) "I was out all night with a beautiful blonde and didn't want to get any sleep."

12) "I was out all night with my wife and couldn't sleep because I kept thinking about the beautiful blonde from the night before."

13) "I can't eat Italian food before I take a lesson."

14) "I can't eat Mexican food before I take a lesson."

15) "I can't eat Chinese food before I take a lesson."

16) "I can't eat a Big Mac before I take a lesson."

17) "I can't eat my wife's cooking before I take a lesson."

18) "I'm hungry and didn't have any lunch before I took this lesson."

19) "I can't run in these horrible sneakers."

20) "I can't run in these horrible Nike sneakers."

21) "I can't run in these horrible New Balance sneakers."

22) "These sneakers are too big for me."

23) "These sneakers are too small for me."

24) "These sneakers are too heavy for me."

25) "These sneakers are too light for me."

26) "These sneakers have no traction and I keep slipping."

27) "These sneakers have too much traction and I can't slide."

28) "This racquet is too powerful for me."

29) "This racquet is not powerful enough for me."

30) "I can't play with this oversize frame."

31) "I can't play with this midsize frame."

32) "The frame you sold me is impossible to control."

33) "You strung this racquet too tight."

34) "You strung this racquet too loose."

35) "I can't play with nylon string."

36) "I can't play with gut string."

37) "I can't play with synthetic gut string."

38) "I can't play with thinner gauge string."

39) "I can't play with thicker gauge string."

cont.

219

40) "I left my good racquet at home."
41) "I left my good racquet in my car."
42) "I left my good racquet in Aruba."
43) "This racquet handle is too big."
44) "This racquet handle is too small."
45) "I need to have Tournagrip on my racquet when I play."
46) "I need to have a cushion grip on my handle when I play."
47) "This grip is too smooth for me."
48) "This grip is too tacky for me."
49) "These courts are too fast for me."
50) "These courts are too slow for me."
51) "I don't play well on Har-Tru courts."
52) "I don't play well on cement courts."
53) "I don't play well on plexi-cushion courts."
54) "I don't play well on grass courts."
55) "These tennis balls are dead."
56) "These tennis balls are too light."
57) "These tennis balls are too heavy."
58) "I can't play with Wilson tennis balls."
59) "I can't play with Pro Penn tennis balls."
60) "The lighting in here is terrible."
61) "The lighting in here is too bright."
62) "I can't play in indirect lighting."
63) "I can't play in direct lighting."
64) "I can't play with these glasses on."
65) "I can't play with these contact lenses."
66) "I can't play without my glasses."
67) "I can't play without my contact lenses."
68) "My knee is killing me."
69) "My back is killing me."
70) "My shoulder is killing me."
71) "My neck is killing me."
72) "My arm is killing me."

cont.

73) "My wrist is killing me."
74) "My knee and back are killing me."
75) "My arm and shoulder are killing me."
76) "My blisters are killing me."
77) "I can't play in the wind."
78) "I can't play in the sun."
79) "I can't play in the cold."
80) "I can't play when it's so hot."
81) "I can't play when it's so humid."
82) "I can't play when it's so hot and windy."
83) "I can't play when it's so sunny and humid."
84) "You hit the ball too slow to me."
85) "You hit the ball too fast to me."
86) "You hit the ball too low to me."
87) "You hit the ball too high to me."
88) "You hit the ball too far away from me."
89) "You hit the ball with too much topspin."
90) "You hit the ball with too much slice."
91) "You're not teaching me properly."
92) "You don't know what the hell you're talking about."
93) "That assistant pro of yours has got me all screwed up."
94) "That pro I took a lesson from in Florida has got me all screwed up."
95) "That pro I took a lesson from in Aruba has got me all screwed up."

221

"I went to Philadelphia over the weekend, but it was closed."

– W.C. Fields

Reality Check #1

It took a recent trip to visit my family and friends in the land of cheesesteaks and Tastykakes to set me straight about one of the most perplexing mysteries from my past. For years I had actually thought that my father really did take my Bar Mitzvah money and secretly invest it in a forest of fruit trees near Tel Aviv. For years, I truly believed that this comic conversation that we always had concerning the hard-earned cash I never saw from this seminal event in my life was actually the truth.

"Let me set you straight, little brother," my sister informed me last time I was in town when my dad and I started our eleven-thousandth exchange on the subject.

"That Bar Mitzvah money you're always joking about that you never saw? Well, rest assured, it went to good use."

"What do you mean?" I asked innocently enough.

"Boy, are you in denial! It's unbelievable! Remember that time – I think it was after your sophomore year in college

– your drunken friends, and you – around 3 a.m. thought it would be a good idea to crash that private party at the big house on the golf course?"

"Oh yeah... I remember now! We were so out of it!"

"And you will recall this triggered a little encounter between you and the Abington Police?"

"Oh man, I thought Dad was going to leave me in the lock-up all night."

"Jesus didn't take care of you that night. It was dad who hired a lawyer to keep you out of jail."

"Right! I had forgotten about that. What year did you say that was again?"

223

"What's the difference, remember little brother... most lawyers don't work for free. Know what I mean!?"

Reality Check #2

It took a recent lunch with my son to recognize another important truth about my life and my waistline.

"I'm ready to diet, son. I'm ready to lose some weight."

"Dad..."

"No really – this time I mean it!"

"Dad – please."

"I'm serious. I'm going to cut out pasta and bread and desserts and…"

"Dad, stop. It's embarrassing. You're in such denial!"

"What do you mean?"

"You've been talking about losing weight for ten years. We both know it's never going to happen!"

"This time will be different! I'm tired of looking like the Pillsbury Doughboy!"

"So this time is going to be different, huh? Okay – let's see. What are you doing for dinner tonight?"

"Tonight? Well, we were going out with a couple of friends to a great restaurant…"

"And naturally you're going to have a couple of bottles of wine like you always do, right?"

"Well, maybe just a few glasses…"

"Uh huh. And what are you going to have for dinner?"

"I hear the restaurant has great risotto and…"

"No, Dad, salad! Have a salad!"

"And I hear they have a great filet mignon…"

"Chicken or fish! Chicken or fish!"

"I know, I know…"

"Dad, unless you change your eating habits – unless you're willing to change the way you live practically every night of your life, you'll never lose weight."

"Alright, alright! I hear you! Let's start right here, right now. Today is the beginning of the new me. I'm going to commit myself to losing ten pounds no matter what! Nothing is going to stop me. I'm going to prove it to you, to myself, and to the world that I can be disciplined enough to say 'No!'"

"That's the spirit, Dad! Great – so let's have lunch. I'm going to start with a salad, and you?"

"Hmmm… I don't know. I'm kind of in the mood for a cheeseburger…"

Reality Check #3

And finally, I had always believed that I was good enough and that I had enough talent to play the world professional tennis tour. It just was not my fault that they failed to invite me to Wimbledon…

"I didn't start playing tennis until I was fifteen years old," I would continually tell people who asked me why I didn't become a world-class player. "If I had only started younger. I mean Jimmy Connors was three years old when he first picked up a racquet. The only thing I was picking up at that age was my mother's *kreplach*!"

"Boy, are you in denial!" one of my tennis pro friends said to me recently after hearing me tell this to one of my students.

"What do you mean?" I responded a little indignantly, somewhat offended by his remark.

"Danny-boy, it's time you faced the truth. A player with your style was never going to make the tour. Have you seen anybody out there who could only slice and chip the ball?"

"Well, no I guess not…"

"Is there any world class player in the last twenty years you can think of who could only push and chop the ball like you, who was consistent and could play great defense but didn't also have the ability to play offensively with topspin?"

"I suppose not…"

"That's right. It's time to face reality. Your game was always going to be good enough to handle the top club players, the Mr. Levines of the world. It was never going to be good enough to beat the Andy Roddicks."

Of course, my friend was right.

And so was my son.

And so was my sister.

Facing the truth is never easy. I wonder what my friend Jack Daniel's would have to say about this?

So I've sorted these things out. I've connected the dots, gotten in touch with my feminine side, come to grips with reality, and accepted responsibility for the consequences of my behavior. And in sharing these adventures I hope I have offered you a few chuckles and a smile or two at my expense. But if for any reason you failed to see the humor in my struggles, couldn't find the wisdom in my tennis tips, or didn't find my journey amusing at all, well, bubby, all I can say is…

227

It's not my fault!

About the Author:
Daniel Waintrup, MBA

Dan Waintrup is a piece 'a work. How is it possible for one human being to be this lucky? He was the toast of his high school and college tennis teams, the drinking buddy of everyone who mattered, and gave heart palpitations to the girls who couldn't get enough of his irreverent side commentary. After a stunning defeat in a major competition sidelined him from national competitive play, he got a plumb job in an exclusive country club where he partied and flirted his way into the social elite of New England's business community. His father, the Rabbi, wailed and prayed and asked God where he went wrong. You didn't do anything wrong, Rabbi, your son is blessed with "the happy gene," and he got it from you.

Dan later completed an MBA and is now affiliated with a New York-based investment company. His social connections brought him face-to-face with the woman of his dreams, to whom he is now happily married. They live in a beautiful home in Brookline, MA, and travel the world. He drives a Mercedes convertible and knows the difference between a goal and a fantasy. He's achieved his goals.

His most recent goal was the completion of this book. With its publication, he has found his true calling. What's next? The movie, the sitcom, the musical? Who knows... But rest assured there's more where this came from. Fasten your seat belt; Mr. Waintrup is on a roll!